Norman Handy was born in Beckenham in the southeast of England. He went to Clare House School and secondary school at a mixed boarding school in Cranbrook, Kent, then university in Southampton to take courses in Law for Accountants, Business Economics and Accountancy.

During his studies, he also travelled as often as he could, such as cycling down La Loire Valley and behind the Iron Curtain. After leaving university, he lived and worked abroad, ending up on a date plantation for a season. He returned to the United Kingdom and after working in a riding school, followed a career in the financial services sector based in London but including periods working aboard in Europe, the Middle East and Asia.

He has two children and is a keen walker, skier, cyclist, horse rider and of course writer! Norman spends his time between his homes in West Sussex and travelling.

Norman Handy

CAPE TO CAIRO

AUSTIN MACAULEY PUBLISHERS

LONDON * CAMBRIDGE * NEW YORK * SHARJAH

A CIP catalogue record for this title is available from the British Library.

ISBN 9781035863822 (Paperback)
ISBN 9781035863839 (ePub e-book)

www.austinmacauley.com

First Published 2024
Austin Macauley Publishers Ltd®
1 Canada Square
Canary Wharf
London
E14 5AA

Table of Contents

Chapter 1
Giant Sand Dunes

When the white missionaries came to Africa, they had the Bible and we had the land. They said, let us pray, and we closed our eyes. When we opened them, we had the Bible and they had the land.
Desmond Tutu

Knowledge without wisdom is like water in the sand.
Guinean proverb

I got a taxi from my apartment not far from the Waterfront in Cape Town to get to the Salty Crax Backpackers Lodge in Tableview, just a twenty-minute journey up the coast by car. I shared the taxi with Sarah, Mat, Laura and Jacci, who were also staying nearby, so rather than take two taxis, we met up at a local restaurant for lunch and then ordered an Uber. It was just a short local journey, but it was the first leg of my journey to get from Cape Town to Cairo overland with a group of friends.

At Salty Crax Backpackers Lodge, I met up with some familiar faces, most of whom I had first met in Morocco. There was Mike, Kenny, Stefano, and Conall, all of whom I had not seen since we were in Cameroon a couple of months previously.

Newbies to the group who I had not met previously were David and Heather, Americans; he was a currency trader and she was a nurse. Kristin was Australian and worked in retail, Zac was from Australia, James was from the Peak District, a self-employed electrical engineer, and Chris, who I had travelled with through Central Asia, was a construction engineer who was between jobs.

We had a meeting to introduce ourselves to each other. I already knew half the group had travelled with them on previous trips. We would be travelling in a converted Scania truck. By tradition, all overlanding trucks have a name, and we were all introduced to Nala and where we would be stowing our stuff in lockers.

I woke up early, but we weren't leaving until 10am to make it an easy first day's drive. Salty Crax didn't serve breakfast, so I walked the short distance from the hostel to the centre of town and the seafront. I found a café and ordered a poached egg on toast. I had a complimentary coffee and walked along the beach before returning to Salty Crax.

We all got on board and set off northwards. The route would go up most of the east coast of Africa to reach Cairo, but first we would be visiting Namibia for some safaris in several game parks before turning east via landlocked Botswana and Zimbabwe and then turning north up the east coast.

As we drove northwards up the South African coast, we passed irrigated fields in the valley bottoms, smoothed into undulating fields to make it easy to use agricultural machinery and not as nature had made it. Where there is water, then there is irrigated fields, and some of this area comprises, the largest grape growing areas in the world, although other fruits are also grown. This area is the heart of the wine-producing areas of South Africa, such as Stellenbosch and the Olifants River.

We stopped at the Highlanders hostel, which is a backpacker lodge, camp site, and small vineyard just outside Klawer. It is a small operation with less than ten hectares of vineyards, but one of the attractions of the place is that they do wine tastings, and we all signed up for a tasting session that evening. There were six wines, one white, three reds, a sweet dessert wine, and a digestif, a strong locally distilled spirit. It was a busy evening as other tour companies had guests at the campsite, and the tasting session was crowded. The young and enthusiastic manager, Morno, is a character and is very good at explaining about the wines.

Not only does he talk through the style of the wine, but he also has a few interesting anecdotes. But people with a fear of dogs should be warned that there were two large dogs that roamed around the campsite and farm buildings at will. Morno introduced them as Bee, a Rhodesian Ridgeback aged three years old, and Jeffery, a Hungarian Vizsla not even a year old.

The Rhodesian Ridgeback is also known as the African Lion Hound. They are muscular dogs weighing up to 45 kilos, used for hunting, and will keep a lion at bay from a camp site. It is called a ridge back from the ridge of hair running along its back in the opposite direction from the rest of its coat and a fan-like area formed by two whorls of hair (called "crowns") behind the shoulders, and the ridge tapers down to the level of the hips. They are loyal, intelligent, and good-natured, and they make excellent guard dogs.

The Hungarian Vizsla is a sport dog but also a loyal companion, related to the pointer and retriever breeds. It is used as a hunting dog for fowl and upland games. They are lively but also gentle-mannered, affectionate but also fearless, and possess a well-developed protective instinct, so they make good guard dogs. They were both good-natured, got along well together, and were tolerant of the constant flow of strangers, but everyone was warned not to feed them.

The night sky was clear and ablaze with shooting stars, and the warm glow of our campfire made for an unforgettable camping experience. It was a clear night, with clear skies all night but in the morning, it was cold and there were clouds at the bottom of the valley. The other guests got up early and left whilst we had a lie-in and a leisurely breakfast before stowing everything away on the truck and setting out. As we moved north, the fields petered out, and it was just rough mountains and valleys with dried-upriver beds and only a few struggling trees. There were a few fields of what must have been wheat, harvested long before, but they were bare and awaiting cultivation for the planting of their next crop.

We crossed the bridge over the Orange River, which forms the border between South Africa and Namibia. The river was named not for the colour of the water but in honour of the Dutch monarch and his family, William V of the House of Orange, by the Dutch explorer Robert Jacob Gordon, commander of the Dutch East India Company garrison at Cape Town, who discovered the river on a trip to the interior in 1779.

There were the usual grumpy border officials who seemed to never smile except one of them, who, in complete contrast, was smiling and asked questions about how we were enjoying our trip as if he were really interested in where we were going, how long we had been travelling, and so on.

We crossed into Namibia, which was discovered and mapped by Portuguese navigators such as Diego Cam in 1485 and Bartolomeu Dias in 1486, but the area was not claimed or colonised by them. Walvis Bay, a large natural deep-water harbour, was occupied by Cape Colony in 1879 and later became part of South Africa. But the rest of present-day Namibia was largely desert or savannah and only thinly populated by indigenous tribes.

Some Boer settlers were escaping British rule in South Africa, as was some German and Swedish settlers. During the Scramble for Africa, Otto von

Bismarck, the German Chancellor, claimed the area, which became a German colony in 1884 and was known as German South West Africa.

The Germans ruled the area with brute force and subjected the indigenous people to dispossession, discrimination, and forced labour. The Herero and Namaqua tribes rebelled, and they were brutally repressed by the Schutztruppe, the German colonial army, during the period 1904-1907. This is said to be the first genocide in modern history, with between 50% and 80% of the indigenous tribes killed.

For instance, in the town of Lüderitz, there is a peninsular that is (incorrectly) named Shark Island. Here, Herero prisoners of war were interred in conditions like a concentration camp. It is a desolate, windswept, stony peninsula with no shade and no water. There are dangerous currents offshore, so escaping by sea was impossible, and it was easy for a few German soldiers to guard the fence between Shark Island and the mainland.

It was at Shark Island that German anthropologists Doctor Fischer and Doctor Bofinger conducted eugenic fieldwork, personally decapitating seventeen prisoners, examining the skulls, and weighing the brains as part of their experiments to prove that the Herero and the Namaqua were not humans but a form of sub-species. They also had the support of Heinrich Göring, then the Governor General of German Southwest Africa and father of Herman Göring, the Second World War Nazi commander of the Luftwaffe. The Doctors later went to work in Berlin, where they would have crossed paths with Dr Josef Mengele, who undertook eugenics and medical research at Auschwitz.

The Schutztruppe was never more than 2,000 strong, but when the First World War broke out in 1914, the Germans attacked Walvis Bay and clashed with Portuguese troops along the border with Angola, although Germany did not declare war on Portugal until March 1916 after they had seized several German ships in Lisbon harbour.

During the outbreak of war, South Africa moved to take control of the area but first had to consolidate its control of its own territory. It had only been 12 years since the end of the Second Boer War, and there was still some Boer pro-German support, resulting in the Maritz Rebellion, which had to be contained first. It took allied troops a year to move up from South Africa to capture Windhoek in May 1915, and they only finally defeated the Germans after the Battle of Otavi in July 1915.

South Africa occupied Namibia under a League of Nations mandate, but after the Second World War, when other former colonies were gaining independence, South Africa consolidated its hold over Namibia. The Southwest Africa People's Organisation (SWAPO) created an armed wing in 1966 to fight for independence, which became the People's Liberation Army of Namibia (PLAN) with support from Russia, Cuba, and Angola. Fighting continued until a ceasefire was agreed upon in 1989 and independence was achieved in 1990.

The economy today is very strong, with tourism, agriculture, and mining being the major industries. Mining produces more than 12% of GDP, and diamond mining produces 7% by itself.

Looking at a map of Namibia, you will notice a panhandle stretching for over 450 kilometres from the northeast corner of the country. This is called the Caprivi Strip. It was named after German Chancellor Leo von Caprivi, who negotiated its acquisition from the United Kingdom in 1890. The intention was to give the German colony access to the Zambesi and hopefully to the Indian Ocean downstream, as well as to Germany's other colony in East Africa, Tanganyika. But nobody checked the maps or any explorer's reports, and the Zambesi to the ocean is unnavigable due to the Victoria Falls. Great Britain agreed to the transfer under the Heligoland-Zanzibar Treaty of 1890, in which Germany gave up its interest in Zanzibar in return for the Caprivi Strip and the island of Heligoland in the North Sea.

It was just a short drive from the border to get to the Felix Unite Camp. We arrived on a Saturday afternoon, but the retail alcohol laws mean that Namibia does not sell alcohol on Saturday afternoons or on Sundays, but the country is not dry as bars and restaurants will still serve alcohol.

We had been crossing an arid area with just a few shrubs, but along the edge of the river are flat, irrigated fields. In Namibia, only the Orange and Fish rivers flow all year and provide plenty of water for irrigation. Coupled with the good weather, the ground is intensively cultivated for vines, fruit, and vegetables. It provides locals with jobs and produce to trade.

The campsite is situated on the high banks, overlooking the Orange River. Besides the camp site, there are lodges for hire and a restaurant with a bar overlooking the swimming pool and the river. The campsite also runs Felix United River Adventures, with options for kayaking or canoeing down the river. Those keen to paddle are taken up the river on a bus with kayaks on the back of a trailer and then paddle down the river for the day to get out at the riverside camp site. Multiple day trips are also available. However much it appealed, we were just passing through and staying for just one night.

We left Felix Unite and turned north to Aussenkehr. It was a local village, and it was predominantly single-room huts, square or rectangular, mostly made of reeds. Reed is a cheap building material and is in plentiful supply on the banks of the river. A few huts had corrugated iron sheets, but they were the exception. The only substantial building in the town was a shopping mall with a bank, clothes shop, and a supermarket. We got there early, but it didn't open until 9am. So much for carefully checking the internet before we left, where the stated opening time was advertised as 8am.

We would have rather had another hour either in bed or at the campsite, but we had time to kill. So, Chris decided to have a haircut. The barbers were just a plastic chair under an open sided reed roofed structure with a crude hand-painted sign hanging from the rafters saying 'haircuts'. He ordered a carrot top crewcut.

Whilst I waited for the supermarket to open, I walked along the edge of the town opposite the mall. There were two shebeens, built of corrugated iron sheets without any windows. There were a few vegetable sellers setting up their stalls and a couple of hairdressers, and Maries Beauty Salon. Maries was a solid corrugated iron sheeting rectangle with no windows. The supermarket doors opened exactly at 9am on the dot, and after getting provisions for the next few days, we were soon back on the road.

After Aussenkehr, the tarmac finished, and we were back on the dirt tracks. We threw up great clouds of dust as we drove across the desert. It had rained here recently, and the desert was starting to bloom in some places. The rain had washed dust and seeds into hollows, grass was sprouting some green shoots, and there were patches of a spiky yellow flowered plant.

In some places, the desert floor was just flat sand. The rain hits it, and it doesn't run off, it just soaks into the ground. The water was not sufficiently concentrated to start any seeds germinating, and there were bare patches devoid of any form of vegetation. It would have to rain for a long time for the water to encourage any seeds to grow, and when rain is rare, a long downpour is a very rare event in the desert.

After a two-hour drive northwards, we stopped at the offices of the Namibian Wildlife Reserve-run resort in Hobas, which is the entrance to Canyon National Park, which is part of the much larger Ai-Ais/Richtersveld Transfrontier Park. We paid for our permit to enter the reserve and drove along the road to the viewpoint. There are hot springs at Ai-Ais, but the big attraction here is the Fish River Canyon. This is the second most visited attraction in Namibia. It cuts deep into the plateau, which today is a dry, stony desert, and sparsely covered with a few hardy drought-resistant plants. It is the largest canyon in Africa, at 160 kilometres long, up to 27 kilometres wide, and, in some places, 550 metres deep.

There is a long-distance path, and keen trekkers can walk the 88 kilometre path, usually taking five days, but there are no facilities, so trekkers have to take all their supplies with them, and open fires are not allowed. Due to very high temperatures in summer, and the danger of flooding, permits are only issued between May and September.

Gareth parked the truck at a lookout point high above the canyon's edge. After gazing from the main lookout, I walked along the rim of the canyon, down river, to a point overlooking the river. I had hoped for a better view, but it eluded me. Then it was another two kilometres back to the lookout in the searing heat of the midday sun. It was autumn time; it should be the rainy season and we were some way to the south of the Tropic of Capricorn, but it was still very bright and hot.

We had a couple of hours to walk along the rim of the canyon and marvel at its depth as the river deep below us meandered along the bottom of the canyon. There is a path down to the river, but it was a hot day, and we didn't have a lot of time. If you ventured down, you would have the long, steep trail to get back to the rim.

Gareth drove the truck back to Hobas and on for half an hour and came across a bizarre sight in the middle of the desert. It was the Canyon Roadhouse, a modern looking building, but it must have been built to supplement the older sheds and garages that surrounded it. There was a collection of old cars and a garage workshop related to paraphilia. A rusted water bore hole drilling vehicle was set up outside the entrance next to the road as a crowd pulled in. Inside the new structure were a bar, restaurant, and reception for some cabins that could be rented overnight. There was no other building as far as the eye could see. The business had seemingly been set up in the middle of nowhere with an old vehicle theme.

Some of the rusted older vehicles had trees growing out of bonnets and boots that must have been at least 40 or 50 years old. Inside was a bar under a large roof that housed a collection of better-preserved old vehicles, with tables set up between the exhibits. It was like eating and drinking in a museum. Outside, when we arrived, there were already two other overlanding vehicles, but inside, it was so large that it could easily hold all of us and not feel crowded.

We set off again across more deserts. We came across a railway line and followed it for a long time, but never saw a train. It had rained recently in the nearby hills, and the riverbeds had been inundated. The water had drained away, but the sand and gravel had been drying for a few days, and there were a few fresh animal footprints in the now dry riverbed.

Then we moved on to a bush camp overlooking the lake formed by a dam on the river. It was an opportunity for a swim, but it was muddy from the recent rains, so it wasn't appealing. It was getting late, and we had jobs to do, such as set up the kitchen, light a fire, put up our tents and find some wood. We cooked over open fires and had a stock of wood, but we always needed more. At every campsite, we would scour the area for wood, but in the desert, there are no trees, just a few shrubs. The thicker pieces are so dry that they burn brightly and quickly, but because they are thin, they don't produce embers or a long-lasting fire.

It was a marvellous sunrise, with the sun rising above the hills on the far side of the lake. The lake glistened, and there was a contrast between the dark hills in shadow, the bright sun and the clear blue skies. There was a lot of debate about what is sunrise and sunset. Was it when the sun was fully up, or was it when the first rays peaked above the horizon? Did the sun set when the leading edge first dipped below the horizon, or was it when it finally disappeared? There were many theories, and several people argued that it was when the sun was totally up and totally down. It was strange how something so straightforward could cause so much heated debate.

I knew the correct answer, but I let the debate flow and take its course before saying anything. Technically, it is when the first rays of the sun peak above the horizon, and that is when the sun rises. The sunset is when the last rays of the sun finally descend below the horizon. But the actual time of sun rise and sun set assumes a smooth globe and depends on the curvature of the earth and latitude. And it ignores the influence of mountains, for instance, so there was still some room for debate depending on local conditions.

As we drove along the road in the morning, we were flagged down by a pickup. It was the owner of a hotel, and one of his guests had forgotten her suitcase and was going on to Swakopmund via the Sossouvlei campsite. He was flagging down traffic to find someone who was going her way. We were going past her campsite and would be going on to Swakopmund. So, both the hotel owner and his former guest got lucky, and we would carry her suitcase all day to reach the Sossouvlei campsite. We telephoned ahead and made a rendezvous at the local garage to return her suitcase.

It was the source of some merriment during the journey as we speculated whether we were, in fact, drug mules. The girls wanted to open the case and check the underwear. Some thought it might be fun to arrive wearing her clothes and deny all knowledge of any suitcase. As it was, it remained firmly closed, and we handed it over to a very relieved woman who was ever so thankful. I would have liked to have known how someone can leave a hotel and not check that you have your luggage.

It was a long drive through the desert. We did a small diversion to stop at the only settlement along the road to get supplies from the supermarket in Maltahöhe. The town was founded in 1899 by Henning von Burgsdorff, a former officer in Schutztruppe who named it after his wife Malta. After getting what we needed for the next few days, we drove out of town and back into the desert. The road ran alongside a private nature reserve and safari lodge. This was an area that seemed to get a little more rainfall or moisture from fog. It was greener and had grass growing in the shade under the few trees that struggled to grow here. We saw some giraffes, Springbok, Steenbok, and Kudu.

We entered the Namib-Naukluft National Park. It covers a huge area, nearly 50,000 square kilometres, larger than Switzerland or Maine and New Hampshire. It comprises the Naukluft Mountains, part of the Namib Desert, and some of its coastline. The Sossou River flows from the mountains and through a canyon, taking sediments towards the coast, but it only flows when there has been sufficient heavy rain. There is more moisture received in this area from fog rolling in from the sea than from rainfall.

Further south along the coast, the Orange River empties into the Atlantic Ocean and drops its load of silt. The Benguela Current pushes all this sand and silt northwards along the coast. The local Sossous and Tsauchab Rivers never reach the sea as the sands move along the coast, are blown inland, and form large dunes that cut off the rivers from the sea. The rivers end in a number of salt pans, and the water is evaporated by the sun or seeps away into the thirsty ground.

We stopped at a marvellous campsite inside the national park. It was a flat sandy pitch away from the others with water and electricity. There was another overlanding truck 50 metres away, but no other neighbours for hundreds of metres. We were the furthest from the central shops, bars, and restaurants, and reception probably put us out here, the furthest from the central core, as groups tend to make more noise, but it also meant that on three sides of our pitch, it was just open uninterrupted desert, a few trees, a few clumps of shrubs, an occasional wadi, uninterrupted views of hills, and a great opportunity to see the sun set with gorgeous reds bouncing off the hills.

The gates to the park only open an hour before sunrise, and then it is a 10 kilometre drive to Dune 45. This is one of the largest dunes in the park. The popular thing to do here is to walk to the top to watch the sunrise, with the darkness of night giving way to sunshine and a range of reds and yellows as the sun lights up the huge dunes. The dunes here are the highest in the world, at between 325 metres and 450 metres tall.

We had breakfast at the base of Dune 45 and then left. We were one person short and waited 15 minutes after our planned departure time, but Kenny was late, so we went without him. As we left, we could see him running after us, but we drove on. The plan was to give us sufficient time to walk around Sossousvlei and then move on to our bush camp. Gareth would drop us off and then drive back to collect Kenny later whilst we were viewing the sights. It seemed a bit harsh, but we had a schedule, and we wanted to have enough time to view everything before moving on. It would also ensure future punctuality for all of the group.

The things to see here are the Sossousvlei salt pans and some petrified trees. The name "Sossousvlei" is of mixed origin, "vlei" is Africaans for "marsh" and "sossus" is Nama for "no return" or "dead end" so it roughly means "dead-end marsh". Sossousvlei owes this name to the fact that it is an endorheic drainage basin, i.e., a drainage basin without an outflow for the sometimes-flowing Tsauchab River, cut off from the sea by advancing sand dunes.

Normal vehicles are not allowed further than the Sossousvlei car park. But you can hire a 4x4 to take you four kilometres to the pan and then a 1.1 kilometre walk to see the petrified trees. The drivers are also tour guides and take you to several places. I queued for a 4x4, but there was a long queue, and it wasn't moving very quickly, so I chose to walk. The route was through soft sand, so I got a little more exercise than I expected. Sitting on a truck for day after day is not conducive to maintaining my level of fitness, and I was eating too much and not getting enough exercise, so I was eager to do some walking.

It was hard work walking in the sand, and the heat was building towards midday. Just one kilometre into the walk, I came across several cars parked at the side of the track. Some were hired vehicles or private 4x4s. The drivers had started up the track, but at this particular point the sand was very soft, and there were at least three abandoned vehicles—two from tour companies and another private vehicle—sunk into the sand up to its axles.

I trudged on through the soft sand to the salt pans of Sossousvlei and beyond to the petrified trees. I retraced my steps to return to the car park and got some water before heading off again for the shorter two kilometre walk to Hiddenvlei.

There was no track, and it is a less favoured destination. There were some footprints, but not many people went this way. There were some posts to mark the route, but by a combination of following the posts and other people's footprints, I made my way across the desert and into the dunes. I came across a salt pan, but this wasn't the destination. Judging by the footprints, several people had turned around here. Only a few sets of prints continued to follow the poles up a sand dune into nothingness.

The extra effort was worth it, as I topped a dune and saw a wide valley below me. The bottom was flat and white from the salt that had accumulated here. There were several dead trees standing on the flat plain. In front of me, a huge sand dune blocked 80% of the width of the valley. The spot was already 40 kilometres from the sea, but as the dune advanced, it would eventually dam the valley, and the river that occasionally flowed would now be blocked even further from the sea.

I wanted to take some photos and walk a little further to get the right angles, but time was against me. I had to return to the truck to move on, and I didn't want to be left behind. I got back with just ten minutes to spare, and after walking in the sun all morning, I had caught the sun. I hid in the shade of the truck until it was time to go.

We continued through the Namib-Naukluft National Park towards Swakopmund. We would not get there in one go, but we had booked a campsite. We turned off the road and found the designated camp site. There were several choices, but we needed to find one that was large enough with sufficient pitches to fit us all. We found an unoccupied site and parked and set up our tents and kitchen.

Chapter 2
Cheetah Farm

Kill one man, and you are a murderer; kill a million, and you are a conqueror.
Jean Rostand

Tomorrow belongs to those who prepare for it today.
An African proverb

We drove on to Swakopmund and through it to visit the Cape Cross Seal Colony Reserve on Namibia's Skeleton Coast. The Portuguese navigator and explorer Diogo Cão was ordered by King João II, as part of the search for a sea route to India and the Spice Islands, to advance south into the unchartered regions along the west coast of Africa. Whilst doing so, he chose some particularly salient points upon which to erect a cross called a padrão. A padrão was a large stone cross inscribed with the coat of arms of Portugal that was placed in a prominent position as part of a land claim by numerous Portuguese explorers during the Portuguese Age of Discovery. They were also used as navigation aids as the coastline was uncharted.

These crosses were often destroyed by natives who were resisting the spread of Christianity and the imposition of slavery. This particular area did not become part of the Portuguese colonial empire, as Portugal gave up its rights to the area under the Treaty of Tordesillas in 1494.

The treaty was sponsored by Pope Alexander VI (formerly Rodrigo Borgia of the famous Borgia family) to avoid a conflict between the Portuguese Empire and the Crown of Castile and León), after Christopher Columbus had returned with news of his discovery of the New World. Lands to the east of a meridian from pole to pole, 370 leagues west of the Cape Verde Islands, would be Portuguese. This would include the eastern areas of present-day Brazil that have not yet been discovered. The land to the west would belong to the Crown of Castile and León.

During his second voyage, Cão reached Cape Cross in January 1486. Being the first European to visit this area, he erected a padrão on the point that was later to be called Cape Cross. Just two years later, in 1488, Bartholomeu Dias successfully rounded the Cape of Good Hope as the first European explorer. The original Cape Cross padrão was removed in 1893 by Corvette captain Gottlieb Becker, commander of the SMS Falke of the German Navy, and taken to Berlin. A simple wooden cross was put in its place. The wooden cross was replaced two years later by a rather poor stone replica.

At the end of the 20th century, thanks to private donations, another cross, and a better reproduction of the original one was erected at Cape Cross, and thus there are now two crosses there.

Today, Cape Cross is a protected area owned by the government of Namibia under the name Cape Cross Seal Reserve. The reserve is the home of one of the largest colonies of Cape fur seals in the world. Cape Cross is one of two main sites in Namibia (the other is in Lüderitz) where seals are culled, partly for selling their hides and partly for protecting the fish stock.

The economic impact of seals on fish resources is controversial. Whilst a government-initiated study found that seal colonies consume more fish than the entire fishing industry catches in an average year, the Animal Protection Society's Seal Alert South Africa is obviously biased in the opposite direction, with an estimated less than 0.3% loss to commercial fisheries due to seals. With such a vast disparity between the two studies, someone must have got their sums wrong.

There were seals and noises everywhere, with young pups waiting for their mothers to return and mothers making their way through the colony calling out to their young. Something that the guidebooks don't mention is the accompanying pungent odour, which is remembered by all visitors. The males had long since done their jobs and had set out to sea again, so there were only mothers and infants on shore.

There were a number of waist-high walls around the car park, but there were seals lying in the lee of the walls out of the wind. There were benches positioned for people to sit on to look out to sea, but all of them were favoured positions for seals to lie on, and we had to stand. There were signs warning people to stay away from the seals, but since they were everywhere, we had to walk around them. There were walkways, but the seals had chosen the smooth surface of the walkways to relax on, so we had to take detours across the shingle to avoid them.

After walking around the seal colony for a while, we made our way back into Swakopmund. It is a microcosm of an ordered Germanic township transhipped to Africa. There is as many German spoken here as English. The streets are neat, and tidy and there are trees, flowers, and grass in the central reservation. There were modern individual houses surrounded by manicured gardens with trees and palms for shade. They had garages and cars, which were mostly parked in garages and driveways, and the streets opposite the houses were free of parked vehicles.

The buildings were all neatly painted and well maintained. The roads were set out in a regular grid pattern, and all had their names on signs at every corner. Despite being largely of modern design, there was a distinct Bavarian and Germanic feel. Most of the city is single or two storey with just a few buildings in the central business district being three stories. There were several church spires of Catholic and Lutheran churches. Except for a few street names of famous local African celebrities, you might think that you were in a Bavarian Alpine town on a summer's day.

The town was founded by Major Curt von François in 1892 and was to be the harbour for the colony. It is not an ideal place, but other sites were less suitable, and nearby Walvis Bay, which has an ideal natural and sheltered harbour, was in British hands. Swakopmund was chosen as it was the nearest coastline to the capital, Windhoek, over 350 kilometres inland.

A railway was built to connect the two which was started in 1897 and completed in 1902. There was some urgency in its construction as transport before the railway was built had been by ox cart, but an outbreak of rinderpest killed off all the oxen. Rinderpest is an infectious viral disease of cattle and related species.

Just 70 kilometres outside of the town is the Rössing uranium mine, which is the largest open-cast uranium mine in the world and the fifth largest producer of uranium, producing 10% of world output, making Namibia the fourth largest exporter. For TV and film buffs, the town was used to film The Prisoner, 1955; The Village, 2004; and Mad Max: Fury Road, 2015.

The town is a centre for adventure activities and adrenaline sports. There are scenic flights over the countryside and along the coast. There are acrobatic flights and skydiving for thrill seekers to free fall from 3,500 metres. There is a horse riding along a dried-up riverbed and into the desert. Out amongst the dunes, there is sandboarding, fat tyre mountain biking, and quad biking on offer.

For water lovers out at sea, there are kayaking options along the coast and leisurely relaxing cruises to see dolphins and seals. There are fishing expeditions and anglers can keep everything they catch. The Benguela Current is rich in minerals and wildlife, and there are large sports fish to catch just offshore.

For those less keen on adrenalin sports, there are township tours and tours to see how the different local tribes live traditionally. You can walk along miles of deserted beaches or visit the museum. The Swakopmund Museum has something for everyone: a video presentation on the history of Namibia, archaeology, history, geology, uniforms, photos of the town since its inception, and several reproduction shops with what they sold when they were first established.

There was a detailed history of the development of the town since the first buildings were erected in 1882 (although the town was not formally founded until 1892). There were exhibits on the development of the railways and the mining industry, principally uranium, but also diamond, copper, lead, zinc, precious and semi-precious stones, and a host of other minerals, including my favourite mineral, gold.

Gold was first discovered in Namibia in 1899, but the grade of the ores was low, there was no gold rush, and commercial mining was abandoned. However, gold was discovered near Karibib in 1984, and the Navachab Gold Mine was developed. Ore grades are about 1.5% to 2%, and its annual production is about 65,000 ounces. For years, this was the only gold mine in Namibia, but B2Gold opened the Otjikoto mine in Otjozondjupa in 2007 and has an annual production of over 189,000 ounces.

I walked to the far side of town to visit the Hauptbahnhof, the original old station but now a four-star hotel. The reception area and bar are original and give an idea of how plush the station was when it was first constructed. Then I walked inland to visit the current station. This was built when the original station was sold off and converted into a hotel. But there are no tracks here as the railway had been realigned again, and now this breeze block-built station is standing by itself in an industrial park.

The current passenger station is another four hundred metres further on, but it is only a platform and a couple of ramps. The train track is three metres away from the edge of the platform, and there are reinforcing rods sticking out of the flat concrete. There are three trains a week between Swakopmund and

Windhoek, but since the tracks have been realigned, another station needs to be built. The trains run overnight, so I was not tempted, as I love to travel by train so that I can look out of the window at the scenery, so an overnight journey is unappealing.

For those who just want to relax, there are a multitude of restaurants, cafes, and bars on offer to suit all budgets and tastes. The town attracts a lot of visitors from both the local area and abroad, and it is a popular destination, being Namibia's most visited city destination.

I went for a walk with Noodles and found a vegetarian restaurant that had a range of dishes, was reasonably priced, but was not open in the evening. It was not far from our hostel and located in the former Otavi railway station, which was built on the outskirts of the town.

The Otavi Mining and Railway Company, shortened to OMEG, built a 600 mm narrow gauge railway from the port via Otavi across 567 kilometres of desert to Tsumeb, whose deep mine produces copper, lead, and zinc ores. It is now called the Ongopolo Mine and is owned and operated by a British company.

Construction of the Otavi railway occurred between 1903 and 1906. Construction was interrupted due to the Herero and Namaqua wars and genocide caused by labour shortages and military operations. A 91-kilometre extension was built from Otavi to Grootfontein in 1908. South African troops captured Swakopmund in January 1915, but the Germans destroyed the track as they retreated. As a result, the South Africans built a 1,067 mm gauge track along the same route to Karibib, about a quarter of the original distance to Otavi, to move troops, supplies, and equipment.

The mine closed in 1933 due to the Wall Street Crash and the worldwide collapse of the international economy, but reopened in 1936 as Germany was rearming. It was closed as enemy property in 1940 but reopened in 1946 and still produces ore. An interesting aside is that the railway service was interrupted in 1924 due to a plaque of locusts. Their crushed bodies on the rails meant that there was no traction. The solution was to add steam blowers to blow the locusts off the track.

The tracks have now been lifted, but the building remains and is a vegetarian restaurant and garden centre. I am a vegetarian, but only for medical reasons, to avoid fat in the meat, not for moral reasons. Therefore, I have no trouble with the occasional meat dish, and whenever a menu claims that a particular dish on offer is a regional delicacy, I can't resist. Therefore, that evening, I treated myself to a game platter at Neapolitanas. It is a taste of some of the wild meat available locally. It consists of small steaks of kudu, springbok, eland, and kudu. They were all good, a bit like venison, but the differences aren't so great that I could pass a blind tasting.

After several days of being able to relax or taste some of the adrenalin rushes on offer, it was time to move on. We stopped on the edge of town at the museum, whose central exhibit is the Luther King steam engine, which I had read about at the Swakopmund Museum. It had been unloaded in Walvis Bay, just down the coast. It took three months to drive the 30 kilometres to somewhere near Swakopmund, where it got stuck and was abandoned a century ago. The museum housed a reconstructed engine surrounded by paraphernalia from the period.

After Swakopmund, we moved on to the stunning Spitzkoppe Rock formations from the German for "pointed dome" and the Groot Spitzkop, which is also known as the "Matterhorn of Namibia". This is a group of bald granite peaks, or inselbergs, located between Swakopmund and Usakos in the Namib desert. The granite is more than 120 million years old, and the highest outcrop rises to 1,728 metres above sea level. The Spitzkoppe Mountains will be recognised by film buffs as they were the filming location for 2001: A Space Odyssey, 1968, written by Arthur C Clarke and produced by Stanley Kubrick. The mountains appear in the "Dawn of Man" sequences.

All of the peaks stand out dramatically from the flat surrounding plains. The highest peak is about 670 metres above the floor of the desert below. Spitzkoppe, although not high, has some challenging terrain for climbers and was not successfully scaled to the summit until 1946. However, there are unsubstantiated reports suggesting that the main peak was reached as early as 1904, when a soldier from the Imperial Schutztruppe supposedly soloed the peak and made a fire on the summit. What he may have burned remains a mystery, as there is absolutely no natural fuel of any kind on the upper parts of the peak. The legend also says that he never returned and that his body was never recovered, so if the story is true, his body is still up there somewhere, waiting to be found. And how do we know that he allegedly reached the top and made a fire? I don't like unexplained mysteries, but I have no further information.

The mountain is part of the Erongo Mountain range and was formed over 100 million years ago after the collapse of a gigantic volcano. There are some interesting walks through the mountains, and when accompanied by the compulsory guide, there is a lot of nature to see, and the guide will show those who are interested a lot of local fauna and flora.

For instance, there are a lot of small holes in the ground. There are some that are small, half-moon-shaped holes that are the homes of scorpions. Our guide said that the fat tailed scorpions are harmless, but the thin tailed ones are poisonous and should be avoided. That may be a great way to differentiate, but until you see both together so as to be able to compare and contrast, the knowledge was of only limited benefit.

The guide will take you to some of the overhangs to see some of the special rock paintings of buffalo, rhinoceros, lions, ostriches, and antelope, as well as of people both walking and hunting on all fours. They are not necessarily easy to make out, but after a bit of guidance, you can start making out the different shapes and interpreting the cave drawings for yourself. The scenery all around is striking from every angle, and it is even more stunning as the granite massifs appear red at sunset from the setting sun.

We passed through the Brandberg Mountains in Damaraland. The highest point is the Königstein, German for 'King's Stone', standing at 2,573 metres and covering an area of approximately 650 square kilometres. The name Brandberg is Afrikaans, Dutch, and German for 'Burning Mountain', which comes from its glowing colour, which is sometimes seen in the setting sun. The Damara's name for the mountain is Dâures, which means 'Burning Mountain' from which the first explorers used to rename the mountain in a European language.

We moved on to check out the camp site but saw a new sign. Previously, it was a free bush camp in the middle of nowhere, 20 kilometres from anywhere, and no one was about. This year, there was a camp, and a new house was being built nearby, surrounded by a garden, some plants, paths, and roads marked out by stones. It was community-owned land, and the camp site provided employment to some locals.

We paid a camping fee and set up our tents. There was a toilet facility nearby, but it was a 100 metre walk and not that sophisticated or welcoming, so most of us went into the desert with a trowel. We had arrived early, and it was a wonderful position as it had a great view of the local mountain and the sun setting, with colours pulsating across the bare desert mountain as the sun set. Later, there were clear skies and a bright moon rise.

In the morning, there was a wonderful moon set just before dawn, with a dull glow off to the west, then a bright sunrise in the east and then we left camp and drove north. We passed through a Herero village, where the women were dressed traditionally and selling wooden animals and beads at the side of the road.

It was noticeable that as we went north, there was more precipitation and more bushes, trees, and grass. There was even water in a few of the water courses. The area is a major mining operation, ultimately owned by Gold Fields. It is the largest open pit tin-tungsten mine in the world. The mine produced about 5,500 tons of tungsten per annum with ore grades of just 0.12% tin and 0.08% of tungsten, so it relies on the high price of the metal to remain economically viable to operate. Tungsten is the main product, and tin is produced as a byproduct.

We stopped in Uis, which is the nearest town to the mines. Standing in the town and looking up, there are large white spoil heaps from the mines that dominate the town. Technology has progressed since the mine was mothballed, and now it is worth the effort to reprocess the spoil heaps to recover ore that was discarded when the mine was in operation as being uneconomic to process. It is a small settlement, and since the mine has been mothballed, people have been moving away, and it is getting smaller. It used to be classified as a village, but in the last few years, it has been downgraded to a settlement.

We had stopped here to shop at the supermarket, but it was closed on a Saturday afternoon and all day Sunday, so we would have to cook using whatever we had left in the cook locker, supplemented by tinned goods that we had stashed away. The supermarket may have been closed, but there were still a lot of people about. We were swamped by people trying to sell us various types of gemstones. Namibia is situated on an ancient landmass, and many of the minerals occur at the surface rather than on the tops of mountains or in deep mines, so they are readily available to local touts who can collect them easily and sell them to tourists.

Several of the locals were bushmen who had either come into town for the day or had left their harsh existence in the bush for a more comfortable life in the village. When they had finished trying to sell us bits of rock, they settled down again and talked amongst themselves. It was fascinating to listen to them, as they spoke a bushman language, which has a series of sounds such as clicks, or a sound made by sucking through your teeth, and there are more than three dozen different types of clicks. There is no written form of the language, so other characters are used to indicate what sound of 'click' is being used, such as ! and ǂ. Different clicks on the same word can change the meaning, and depending on the specific click used, one particular word, for example, can mean elephant, spoon, or cat.

We passed giraffes and ostriches and turned off the road after three hours from Uis onto the Otjitotongwe Cheetah Guest Farm. It looks like any other farm in the area, with hundreds of hectares of scrubland and livestock that roam the savannah. But the unusual thing about this farm is that there are cheetahs here, not just in the savannah but up close and personal, and we would have an opportunity to get really close to these amazing and endangered creatures.

The guest area has some camping pitches, a barbecue pit, some cabins, and a swimming pool with trees for shade. We changed and dived into the pool to cool off, then sat under the trees for shade. Among the selection of trees were the perfume tree, used by indigenous people to make perfume, and the paper tree, where the bark can be peeled off in large sheets and can be used straight away as paper.

Weaver birds were nesting overhead, with their carefully weaved nests hanging from the ends of slender branches. They are weaved from grass and have two entrances, but they often only use one habitually. The alternative entrance/exit is to provide an escape route. If a snake crawls up the branch, it will dip with the extra weight, and that is the sign for the birds to use the emergency exit to fly away.

Gareth had pre-ordered a sheep carcass, and the manager brought it over, and we started the fire to cook it slowly over the barbeque. But the highlight of the visit came in the late afternoon, which was feeding time for the cheetahs. Not all of us wanted to go, so Noodles, Gareth, Kim, and Conall stayed behind. They were roasting a whole sheep for our evening meal, and Noodles started the main dish and side dishes for the vegetarians, which were to be chickpea burgers and bean salad.

Meanwhile, we walked up the farm track to the main farmhouse. The house and gardens are surrounded by a tall fence with a large gate with a sign saying 'Ring the bell and wait'. There is also another sign, and I am used to signs warning about guard dogs roaming free, but this sign was warning that there were cheetahs roaming free on the grounds.

It is a family-run farm, owned by the Nel family, and one of the brothers came and opened the gate to let us in. Wandering around the enclosure surrounding the house were three cheetahs. They had been here for a long while since they were cubs and were tame and used to humans. We stood in the lawn, and the cheetahs walked between us, sometimes stopping to sniff and sometimes chasing each other.

There were certain rules for safety. We had been told to keep your face away from their face. You can approach them from behind and pat their backs, scratch their necks, or hide behind their ears, just like domestic cats, but keep away from their paws. Sunglasses were not allowed, as they see their reflection and might react, possibly violently.

There was a tree with some low branches, and the cheetahs climbed up the tree, jumped out, and joyfully played with each other. It is absolutely amazing to stand in the garden and have these predators walk between us. Roeleen, the wife of one of the brothers that runs the farm, was quite confident to walk around her garden and let her two small children play on the lawn, despite the animals wandering about and their reputation as hunters. These were obviously domesticated and considered safe enough for even the children to play unsupervised in the garden.

The cheetahs came over and licked the sweat off people's arms, and whilst you might sit down and watch one, another would come up behind you and lick your neck and ears. Some people were relaxed with the close encounter, but several others kept their distance.

Farmers used to shoot the cheetahs, as they are predators and would prey on the farm's cows, sheep, and goats. Once they find a good source of food, they will stay. Even if they are captured and taken into the hills to be released, they will find their way back and prey on the farm animals again. Therefore, they used to be shot. Now neighbouring farms are capturing wild cheetahs, and Cheetah Farm gets them to look after. It attracts tourists, and many stay at the camp site or in the lodges, so it is another stream of income for the farm.

It was feeding time, and the cheetahs got excited as large chunks of meat were thrown at them, which they caught and then settled down to gnaw at the hunks of zebra meat. After eating, they wandered away, found a spot to relax, and dozed off. It is an expensive operation, but neighbouring farms cooperate. Injured or orphaned cheetahs are captured and taken to the farm. Roadkill and carcasses found on neighbouring properties are donated as food. The other farms in the area benefit as the cheetahs are all located in one area, so their livestock is at less risk of being preyed upon.

Then it was feeding time for the feral cheetahs. We had an up close and personal interaction with some cheetahs who were used to humans. We just took a 4x4 drive into a fenced reserve where there are more than a dozen wild cheetahs. They are fed regularly in the late afternoon and have become accustomed to the 4x4s and humans, but these cheetahs are still feral and might attack, so more precautions are required. We stood in the back of the 4x4s and held on tight, holding on to your cameras, not leaning out, and obviously not leaving the vehicle for any reason.

We stopped nose to tail, and we were circled by the cheetahs. They knew what was coming next, and they had all come to get their share of the meat. Great chunks of meat were pulled out of a dustbin and thrown into the air to be caught by the cheetahs, often before they hit the ground, and carried away to be eaten in peace away from the other cheetahs.

Eventually there was little activity to see as the cheetahs took their catch and lay down in the tall grass to eat their meal, which was time for us to return to the farmhouse. Then we walked back from the farmhouse down the farm track to our campsite and settled down for an evening barbecue of slow roasted barbecued sheep or chickpea burgers for the vegetarians. I felt tired and returned to my tent, where I soon fell asleep. I was awake in the night, and on my way to the toilet, I noticed that Noodles and Conall were still awake, and they stayed up until 4.30am.

Chapter 3
Etosha National Park

The darkest thing about Africa has always been our ignorance of it.
George Kimble

A man who makes trouble for others is making trouble for himself.
Nigerian proverb.

We drove from Cheetah Farm to Outjo and stopped for an hour for the cook groups to shop and for the rest of us to get some snacks and drinks. Several cook groups went shopping as we would be camping for the next few nights, two in Etosha National Park, and then we would cross the border into Botswana, and it would be a couple of days before we would get to our next supermarket. The alcohol tax in Botswana also makes any beer or wine much more expensive, so we stocked up on our choice of beverages in Outjo. There was a security guard at the entrance to the car park in the centre of town, and I wondered what he thought of a lot of white people each coming back to the truck, pushing trolleys loaded with slabs of beer and boxes of wine.

Then it was another drive through the savannah to get to Etosha National Park, and we entered through Anderson's Gate. Explorers Charles John Andersson and Francis Galton were the first Europeans to record the existence of the Etosha pan in 1851. The park was proclaimed a game reserve in 1907 by the Governor of German South West Africa, Dr. Friedrich von Lindequist, who designated it Game Reserve Number 2, in numerical order after West Caprivi, which had already been designated Game Reserve No. 1.

In 1958, the reserve became Etosha Game Park and was upgraded again to a national park in 1967. The name Etosha comes from the local Oshindonga word meaning Great White Place, referring to the Etosha pan. The area is an endorheic basin, meaning that it has no exit for the water. When it rains in the summer, two major rivers empty into the pan, and the lake increases in area, but the water slowly evaporates and shrinks again, leaving a large, flat salt pan.

From Anderson's Gate, we drove to the salt pan and then alongside it, crossing a large grass plain towards our camp site at Halali Camp. We saw impala, secretary birds, elephants, oryx, steenbok, wildebeest, Hartemans zebras, mountain zebras and loads of birds—too numerous to mention. Also, we found a black rhino standing near the side of the road and eating some grass contentedly. We watched it for a while and took loads of photos, but it was getting late, and we had to be at our designated camp site before dusk, so we had to move on.

We passed other potentially interesting sights, including a white rhino and calf, but it was a race to get into the campsite before the gates closed, and you would be fined for driving at night and potentially kicked out of the park. So we drove straight past several giraffes, porcupines, and another elephant to get to camp with just minutes to spare. The gates were closed behind us, and we found our designated site, but we had to put up our tents and cook in the dark, using just the lights from the truck and our head torch.

The camp has a lookout spot overlooking a watering hole, which is fenced for safety and lit up at night so visitors can see the animals. We all went down to the watering hole, but nothing much turned up whilst we were there. However, earlier in the day, there had been reports of warthogs and hyenas who came and went very quickly, and several black and white rhinos. Both come in various shades, but the 'white' is a corruption of the German for being wide mouthed, as it has a wide-mouth and can graze both grass and the leaves on tree branches. The black rhino has a narrow mouth, can only graze and is the more endangered of the two types.

We were up early for a game drive, and the first vehicle in the queue to get out of the camp at sunrise. We went to another watering hole to see the game, but there was not much to see. Most animals can get the water they need from the plants, and as it was the rainy season, they required fewer visits to a watering hole. We talked about seeing the Big Five, the five most difficult large game animals to hunt on foot. These include lions, leopards, rhinoceros, elephants, and Cape buffalo, which are on the big game list to tick off if you go on safari.

This original grouping was so successful with tourists that other groups of five were created. Another group was the Little Game Five, coined by nature conservationists to highlight smaller species and, as a bit of fun, used animals with a similar name but the opposite in terms of size compared with the large game animals. These are the elephant shrew, the buffalo weaver bird, the leopard tortoise, the ant lion, and the rhino beetle. Various commentators have since expanded their range, with some overlap, to include the carnivorous five, the ugly five, and so on.

My target animals were lions and leopards. I had seen lions here before, but they are majestic animals, and I was always happy to see more. My other target was the leopard, but they are elusive. We saw neither, so it was a bit of a disappointment, but there would be other opportunities. We saw impala, springbok, white rhinos, oryx, a secretary bird, and loads of other birds but no leopards.

We spent a long time watching springboks and zebras at several watering holes, hoping for a predator to show up, but there were no leopards or lions. A juvenile spotted a hyena next to the road. They just lay there in the sun and ignored us. Eventually they got tired of the noise of excited tourists on safari and got up and moved away, which was our cue to move on.

We stopped at one of the few places where you can get out of your car in order to go to the toilet. There was also a display board there, so you could check out what animals are usually found in the vicinity. It was also a chance for a mid-morning break since we had got up so early. By lunchtime, we had reached the exit at the far end of the park, and we were hungry, so we left the park and stopped for a truck lunch. This was usually a simple affair, and the cook group would provide bread for sandwiches, some fillings, or perhaps a salad.

Then it was a long drive in the afternoon. We were passing palm trees of various sorts, as this area gets more rain and is well within the tropics, so it was more of what you might expect than an endless desert. But it was still an unending savannah for hours after hours. The area is generally flat, so there are no hills to break up the scenery, and you might not look up from your book or handheld electronic game device, but you were unlikely to miss anything.

We pulled off the road at what used to be the largest baobab tree in Namibia. We parked the truck at the side of the road, and then it was a short walk into the savannah. It was indeed an old, gnarled tree with an impressive girth, but it lost its special status in 2001 when an even larger girthed tree was found elsewhere. It is 30.2 metres in circumference and estimated to be 1,700 years old.

This was also meant to be a bush camp, but the facilities were being upgraded and a campsite was being built. There were large pitches, a large facilities block, and what might eventually be cabins for upgrades. The spare patch of ground was now an entrance to a large campsite, but it was still under construction, and no one was around, so we pitched our camp outside the gates. We had a visitor that evening as a giraffe walked through the camp. He was as surprised to see us as we were to see him, but he just walked on into the distance.

In the far north of Namibia, the savannah receives more rain, and there are trees and some fields, mostly growing maize. There are the traditional round mud huts with roofs made of thatch in neat little compounds of hard, dry, beaten earth. And the roads were good tarmac, so we had a good time and covered a lot of distance. We were driving along part of the Caprivi Strip, a long panhandle of land belonging to Namibia, with Botswana to the south and Angola to the north.

It was a long day driving to reach the border to cross into Botswana. I got a stamp on my passport to leave Namibia, but it took up most of the page. The Botswana official was much more considerate and squeezed my entry stamp into a corner of an already half-full page, leaving enough space to squeeze in an exit stamp as well. With so many countries to visit and many require a visa which can take a whole page, plus entry and exit stamps, my passport would fill up quickly, and passports are expensive, but when it is full, even if it is still valid, I would need another passport, and therefore I would ask officials to make a stamp in a particular place on a page to maximise the space available.

During the Scramble for Africa, the territory of present-day Botswana was coveted by both Germany and Great Britain. During the Berlin Conference, Britain decided to annex Botswana in order to safeguard the Cape Colony and its connection to present-day Zimbabwe and Zambia, formerly called Northern Rhodesia. It unilaterally annexed the Tswana territories in January 1885 and then sent the Warren Expedition north to consolidate control over the area and convince the chiefs to accept British rule, and it became the British protectorate of Bechuanaland.

Botswana adopted its new name after becoming independent within the Commonwealth in 1966. The country's name means "land of the Tswana", referring to the dominant ethnic group in Botswana. It has maintained a strong tradition of stable democracy, with a consistent record of uninterrupted democratic elections and the best perceived corruption ranking in Africa since at least 1998, which is unusual since many of the former colonies and now independent countries in Africa have made very difficult history on the path towards self-governance and corrupt free administration, which is the preferred goal, but many countries are still on the journey decades after independence.

Botswana is topographically flat, with up to 70 percent of its area being the Kalahari Desert. It is a large country, but with just over 2 million people, it is one of the most sparsely populated countries in the world. Formerly, it was also one of the poorest countries in the world, with a GDP per capita of about USD70 per person per year in the late 1960s. Botswana has since transformed itself into one of the world's fastest-growing economies. The economy is based on agriculture, largely cattle, and tourism, but these sectors are dwarfed by the mining industry, dominated by diamonds, gold, uranium, copper, and nickel, which are, money-wise, very important but don't necessarily employ a large proportion of the population.

Botswana's Orapa mine is the largest diamond mine in the world in terms of value and quantity of carats produced annually. It is estimated to have produced over 11 million carats in 2013, with an average price of USD145 per carat. The Orapa mine was estimated to have produced over USD1.6 billion worth of diamonds in 2013. The name of the mine, Orapa, means "resting place for lions". It is owned by Debswana, a partnership between the De Beers Company and the government of Botswana. It is the oldest of four mines operated by the company, having begun operations in July 1971.

Botswana now boasts a gross domestic product per capita of about USD 18,825 per year as of 2015, which is one of the highest in Africa, and its gross national income is the fourth largest in Africa. But it is not all good news because, as of 2014, Botswana has the third-highest prevalence rate for HIV/AIDS, with roughly 20% of the adult population being infected.

We were looking for a bush camp and found an unlikely spot. Disappearing into the savannah was a partially made road. The vegetation had been cleared and a gravel base had been laid, but the project had been abandoned. There were piles of gravel ready to be used, but there were plants and shrubs growing out of both the gravel piles and out of the gravel that had been laid to create the base of the road. We made ourselves at home, collected some wood from the surrounding savannah, and set off again shortly after dawn.

We stopped for a break to stretch our legs, for lunch, and to go shopping in Maun. Then it was time to check into the Okavango River Lodge. The Okavango Delta is one of the world's largest inland deltas, formed when the Okavango

River, fed by rains in the highlands and jungles of Angola, reaches the central part of the endorheic basin of the Kalahari. Each year, during the rainy season, about 11 cubic kilometres of water spread over the 6,000-15,000 square kilometres of the delta. Some flood waters flow past Maun to drain into Lake Ngami or further afield and into Lake Makgadikgadi in Makgadikgadi National Park to the southeast of Maun.

Chapter 4
The Okavango Delta

Every mountaintop is within reach if you just keep climbing.
Barry Finlay

Wisdom is like the baobab tree; no one individual can embrace it.
Akan proverb from West Africa.

The Okavango Delta was named one of the Seven Natural Wonders of Africa, which were officially announced in 2013 in Arusha, Tanzania, and the next year, the Okavango Delta became the 1,000th site to be officially inscribed in the UNESCO World Heritage List. People are familiar with the Seven Wonders of the Ancient World, even if most people can't name all seven. However, I did have to look up the Seven Natural Wonders of Africa, the other six being.

1) Red Sea Reef off the coast of Egypt, Eritrea, and Sudan
2) Mount Kilimanjaro, Tanzania
3) The Sahara Desert, which is spread across Algeria, Chad, Egypt, Libya, Mali, Mauritania, Morocco, Niger, Sudan, Tunisia, and the Western Sahara
4) Serengeti Migration between Tanzania and Kenya
5) Ngorongoro Crater, Tanzania
6) The Nile River, which flows through Uganda, South Sudan, Sudan, Ethiopia, and Egypt with headwaters in the Democratic Republic of the Congo, Kenya, Tanzania, Rwanda, and Burundi, which is the world's longest river.

In order to get to the Okavango River Lodge, we drove over some rough dirt tracks to get to the river's edge, but this was not where the lodge was located. The lodge was deep in the delta, and we would have to take several canoes up river to get to the lodge.

We were introduced to our guides and cooks. Our guides were Costa Rica and Bush Ranger, which were both his name and his job. The rest of the team were Terence, Hansa, Diks, Otis, Natasha, Kathryn, and Jessica. We unloaded the truck and trailer and transferred everything into canoes. Our tents went in one canoe and our food and cooking equipment went into another, our bags into a third. We split into pairs, and with our day packs, we got into the canoes. Except for the luggage canoes, there were two people per canoe with their day packs and a member of the team to pole us up the river.

We passed through the Buffalo Fence. There is some excellent grazing land on one side of the fence, but the tsetse fly is a problem for both domesticated cattle and wildlife. The fence was to keep the domesticated cattle out of the delta area in an attempt to keep the wildlife and the domesticated animals separate and limit the spread of the tsetse fly. There was also a problem with foot and mouth and so a huge fence has been erected around the majority of the Okavango Delta, some neighbouring areas, and despite local opposition, it was a great success. And success is a rare event on a continent where so much aid had been squandered to achieve very little.

We hadn't gone far when the lead canoe called a halt. There were four elephants standing in the reeds at the edge of the waterway. We had to wait whilst they waded across. We couldn't see them until we were quite close to them, as we were low down in the canoe and the reeds were two metres high and thick. They bellowed and flapped their ears as a warning, but after we stopped, they sensed that we were not a threat and calmed down. Then they crossed the waterway, and we had a good view as they waded through the open water ahead of us.

The preferred method of moving through the delta is by poling rather than by paddling. Paddlers would be low down and might miss the wildlife until they were almost on top of each other. By standing and poling, the polers get a view across the reeds and can see the elephants. They can also sometimes see and avoid the hippopotamus. These are the most dangerous animals in Africa, and they kill more people than any other animal.

People can see large wild animals and can avoid them. Hippopotamus dislike the sun as their skin is subject to sunburn, so they spend most of the day submerged in water with just their ears, eyes, and/or noses exposed. They can stay under water for five minutes, so they may be there, and you can't see them. They are also territorial, and whilst they are vegetarians, they have an attitude, and if you get too close, they will attack.

We waited whilst the elephants crossed the shallow channel, but the last one, a juvenile male, crossed and walked parallel to the watercourse and towards us. He turned his head towards us and flailed his ears at us. This is a warning sign and the start of a mock charge to warn us to stay away, but there is not much that we could do as we were in canoes and limited to the channel, but we inched sideways and backwards away from him as best we could. The young male flailed his ears a couple more times and then walked on to follow his companions, and we were able to continue up the river.

It was a pleasant pole up the river, and we stopped for a break near a little mound. From the top, we had a good view across the flat delta, some of the islands, and the horizon dotted with trees and palms. During the rainy season, much of this area is flooded with only a few islands pocking through the waters, but at this time of year, the water was restricted to a few channels and shallow pools.

A few of the local sights were pointed out, such as the fauna and flora of the delta. One in particular struck me. It was a small frog crouching on the stem of one of the tall reeds, waiting for some lunch to come past. What was odd was that it was white and not very well camouflaged at all. But there were so many white lilies flowering on the surface of the water that it blended into the background quite well.

Local guides and polers navigated the extensive waterways using canoes similar to their traditional Mokoro, or dugout canoes made from hardwood trees and hollowed out by hand. This is a great experience and the best way to have a chance of seeing the elusive wildlife of this unique desert oasis. After a few hours of moving through the reeds, we beached the canoes and started unloading. We set up our tents and the kitchen. It was a shaded spot on some high ground overlooking one of the many fingers of the Okavango River as it splits, subdivides, and spreads its thin fingers of water across the flat landscape.

One of the guides dug a deep hole behind a bush to serve as the toilet. There was a piece of string on one side that acted as the red-green indicator on public toilets. If the string was tied across the path leading to the hole in the ground, it was an indicator that someone was using the facility. We sat in the camp as it was too hot to go anywhere, and we wrote diaries, played cards, and talked over cups of tea or some cold beers from the cool box that we had brought with us and had filled with enough ice to last several days.

After the heat of the midday sun had passed, we went for an afternoon safari walk into the delta. We split into two groups. Costa Rica was led by one, whilst Hansa and the Bush Rangers led the other with Terence. The heat of the day had gone, and there was a pleasant, clear sky. We walked past one of the three baobabs on the island. They stand in a row, and you can just about see one from the other. Therefore, if you were ever lost, we could find the camp by finding the baobab trees.

We saw giraffes in the distance, easy to see as their heads were above the tree canopy. We caught sight of the rear of an elephant before it disappeared into the trees. Out on the grasslands, there were several groups of zebras. They like the open plains as there is plenty of grass, and they can keep an eye out for predators. They could also see us coming, and they moved on, led by a dominant female. As the sun set, we made our way back to the camp.

We had had a great day, and there was a party mood in the camp. We usually cooked for ourselves, but part of the attraction of this experience was that we had cooks, Otis, Natasha, Kathryn, and Jessica from the local village, so they were peeling, slicing, and boiling, and we all had the evening to enjoy ourselves and relax. We had aperitifs, played cards, and chatted. It was billed as a lodge, but it was a camp site, and everybody had been warned that we would be sleeping under canvas.

Those who were more concerned about the wildlife pitched their tents near the fire. Some of us were bolder and pitched our tents further away from the fire, but it also meant that we were on the outskirts of the camp and would be more likely to have our first encounter with wildlife. It was an anxious moment and comical looking back on it as if you needed to get up during the night and heard a noise. Was it a prowling lion and you would be a lion's early breakfast, or was it one of the groups having a pee behind a bush? There were a few close encounters and nervous moments, but no dangerous encounters with predators.

We woke up before dawn to have a hot drink before setting out on a dawn walking safari. There were two groups led by the same rangers as last night: Costa Rica and Bush Ranger. The dull red glow of the rising sun burst into bright sunlight as it peaked above the horizon. There were herds of zebras grazing on the open plain, and I learnt that the collective noun for zebras is dazzle. There were a few wildebeests among them—not a herd, but just a couple each by themselves. Wildebeest benefit from zebras' collective concern for the security of the herd and their constant watch for predators. Zebras like the burnt-out patches of grass, as after a fire has cleared the old growth, the grass will regrow with fresh shoots a couple of weeks later that the zebras like.

As we watched them, flight after flight of white pelicans flew low overhead. They were setting out from their roosts to fly to some lagoons, where they would feed all day before making the return journey before nightfall.

Pocking out above the tall grass were the tops of termite mounds. They are as deep underground as they are high above ground. Some were in use, and new tunnels on the outside could be seen, which would have been made overnight. They are the favourite food of anteaters and aardvarks. The mounds are abandoned after a sustained attack, and the termites will start another mound. Even the abandoned mounds are surprisingly strong despite being just made of soil and spit and left abandoned for the weather to erode them. It is also a useful resource for villagers to use the mud from abandoned mounds to make mud bricks for building their huts, and despite the rainfall, the bricks are also surprisingly resistant to rain and erosion if the roof is well made.

Some of the flora was pointed out, such as the red apple, although it is not edible for humans. Also, the sausage tree, which grows to over 20 metres tall and has long green fruits like giant cucumbers or sausages. Fruits are hard and heavy, and weights of over six kilogrammes are quite common throughout the area. Therefore, this is a bad tree to walk under or to camp under. The fruit is believed to cure snake bites, rheumatism, and syphilis in traditional medicine. And because of its importance to local customs, it is not common to cut down this tree species.

Opposite this specimen was a Rain Tree, which attracts a certain bug that eats the leaves and poops every five seconds, so if the tree has an infestation, there is a constant sticky rain fall, and this is another tree to avoid walking or camping nearby.

As we walked across the ground towards a water hole, we came across an egg snake. It was immobile, and on closer inspection, it was dead as it had been caught in a wildfire and whilst not burnt as it had stayed close to the ground.

There was also fresh elephant dung, which takes the form of great balls of partly digested coarse grass the size of footballs, and the foot marks were clearly visible, but their passage was given away by the fresh piles. Looking at the footmarks of the elephants and the way they had gone, we could see three in the distance. Then all of a sudden, we saw several Red Lechwe, a type of aquatic adapted antelope who have webbed feet that use the wetter areas to escape from predators who can't follow them.

Then we came across some hippopotamus tracks. They move between lagoons during the night and use the same pathways. With constant usage, they eventually wear a wide trench through the undergrowth, which can be ankle deep. We reached the lagoon, and there were two groups of hippos. There were the sounds of occasional honks as they called to each other and alerted us and each other to their presence.

All you could see were their eyes, ears, and noses above the water. Several surfaced and floated near the surface or dived, but once they had seen us, they turned to face us. Some came close over the course of an hour, and one rushed forward. It was a mock charge, but we stood our ground. Standing together makes us look larger and may deter the hippopotamus from charging, but a single person who turns and runs could be overtaken by the hippo and trampled to death. But it did mean that we were too close, and they weren't happy with our presence, so it was time that we backed off and moved on.

We were walking through the savannah and came across a herd of giraffes, but I didn't know until Bush Ranger told us that a collective noun for giraffes is a tower of giraffes. We already knew that it was a dazzle of zebras, but there was also a crash of hippopotamus, and a knot of snakes. There were several giraffes, including some youngsters. We had disturbed them, and they ran away, but they are amusing when they run as both legs on the same side move together, and it looks like a very unusual gait. There was also a troop of baboons in some trees off to one side, calling to each other. We watched for a while until they moved away to forage in some trees further away from us.

We walked on, and we were approaching our campsite. As we neared the camp, there were several elephants between us and our destination. There was no alternative path, so we just had to wait until they moved on. We watched for a while until they moved away, and then we were able to get back to camp.

Then it was time to chill out for the rest of what was left of the day. It was hot, and it seemed like a good idea to go for a swim. We heard hippopotamus honking during the night upstream, so it would be best to avoid that area. We also needed some shallow water where we could see the bottom and know for certain that there were no crocodiles, hippopotamus or anything else in the water to harm us. The preferred swimming spot is a short canoe ride away, so we got ready and set off in the canoes.

The only problem was that three elephants had the same idea, and they were splashing about in our proposed swimming spot. They were clearly enjoying it, and we waited in the canoes a short distance away whilst they drank and splashed. But it seemed like they weren't going to move on quickly. After an hour of waiting, no one liked the idea of swimming as the water would be churned up, muddy, and there would be elephant poo in the water, so after that hour, we turned around and went back to camp without having a swim.

Some of us had a quick splash near where we had drawn the canoes up the bank. It was shallow and closed in with reeds and our guides were nervous. They didn't stop us, but from the way that they scanned the reeds, and waded into the water, calling to each other and beating the reeds with long sticks, it wasn't a safe place, so no one stayed in the water for very long.

We had another late afternoon walk to see the sun set, to see some of the pelicans returning, but not in the great flights that we had seen in the morning. I couldn't go on the walk as the chefs had the evening off and I was cooking with Chris and Noodles. We cooked lentil curry for the vegans and vegetarians and beef curry for the meat eaters.

There was a sun rise tour, and those of us who were up early saw more zebras, more elephants, pelicans, and a totally clear sky to watch the sunrise. We returned to camp for breakfast. We packed up and took everything in camp back down to the canoes. We loaded the cooking equipment, the tents, and our bags into the canoes, and after checking that nothing was left on our camp site, we got into the canoes.

It was an easy trip back to the mainland, going downstream with the current. We didn't get stopped by elephants, and we didn't stop to get out to stretch our legs. The only stop was a pause to take photos of a fish eagle perched high in a tree, watching us and looking out for fish.

We got back to the launch point a few days ago and unloaded the canoes. We loaded all our tents, cooking equipment, and bags onto the truck to take everything back to the local hostel. When we got back to the hostel, we unpacked everything, washed it all in hot water, and then dried and packed everything away again back, in its proper places on the truck.

We also met up with fellow members of the group who had not accompanied us into the Okavango Delta, such as Kenny, who had had his own story about close encounters with crocodiles on the river when he had taken a small boat by himself down the river in front of the hostel.

Then we sorted out our own bags to repack them onto the truck. We set off and drove for the afternoon northeast towards Kasane in the far north of the country. Enroute, we saw several elephants walking in a line near the road. It goes to show how many elephants we have now seen, as we haven't stopped and we haven't even slowed down. No one pushed the buzzer to stop the truck or to take photos. Some people didn't even look up, as if it were now as common as seeing cows at home.

Chapter 5
Zimbabwe

Wood burns faster when you have to cut and chop it yourself.
Harrison Ford

If you think you are too small to make a difference, you have not spent a night with a mosquito.
African proverb

The road was tarmac and a major route, but there was little traffic, so we made good progress. We had a bush camp not far from the road. Our chosen site looked good during the late afternoon, but it was an insect infested nightmare at night.

All of us were only too glad to move on in the morning. I called this Waterhole Camp in the absence of any other name as it had several pools adjacent to the approach track to the grassy flat area set back from the road. It looks like an ideal bush camp location, but we will learn later how deceptive it can be.

The night was bad with insects, but the morning had a heavy dew. It was cool and damp, but at least it was free of insects. We made good use of the chainsaw and chopped up enough dead wood to fill the wood lockers for the next few days, as we knew that we would be unable to find wood in Zimbabwe. There is wood, but the roads are fenced, and the country is densely populated, and the locals pick up any wood for their fires, so we would be very lucky to pick up wood for free in Zimbabwe.

We headed east to Nata and turned north to reach Kasane, just outside Chobe National Park. We had lunch at the campsite, which was part of the upmarket Chobe Safari Lodge, posh but affordable. We set up our tents, and then that afternoon we gathered at the bar, ready to go for a boat safari on the Chobe River the Chobe National Park.

We walked down to the river's edge and were directed to a small boat. There were several boats and several queues, but we had a boat just for our group. The captain cast off, motored upriver, and stopped at the ranger's hut on the top of the bank at the entrance to the park to pay our entrance fee.

From the comfort and safety of the boat, we saw elephants, crocodiles, fish eagles, cormorants, and hippopotamus by the score. A pair of Egyptian geese were standing on the bank just a metre from a crocodile, seemingly oblivious to its presence. If they got any closer, they would be the crocodile's dinner. We watched more hippopotamuses swimming in the water. We utilised the bar on the boat and had a great afternoon. We watched the sun set, and then we had to exit the park before dark. The hippopotamuses were now less easy to see as they were in the water, and the captain would point one out, and then it would submerge.

There were refreshments on the boat, and we helped ourselves as the captain navigated up the river. We reached the upstream tip of Kasikili Island, which sits in the middle of the river. It was the subject of a long-running dispute between Namibia and Botswana due to the imprecise wording of the border treaty between the British Protectorate of Bechuanaland and German-controlled Sout West Africa signed in 1890. It was only resolved by the International Court in a ruling in 1999 that it belonged to Botswana. It is only a few square kilometres and is submerged during the rainy season when the river floods, so it was never a serious bone of contention, but it did need an authoritative resolution.

We had to be out of the park before sunset when the park closed so we motored down the Zambezi on the northern side of the island. We saw a wonderful sunset as we passed the downstream tip of the island and then motored back to our campsite at the Chobe Safari Lodge.

Gareth and Kim had stayed behind at the camp site and had cooked an evening meal over a barbecue for us. Although the camp was fenced, there were still schools of mongoose and the occasional warthog wandering around inside the perimeter fence and crocodiles and hippopotamus down by the water's edge, so you still had to look out for wildlife. It was allegedly secure, but you still had to exercise care and attention.

It was a noisy night with hippopotamuses honking, cicadas chirping, things rustling in the bushes, cockerels crowing, and then the birds started singing to herald the dawn. We crossed the Botswana-Zimbabwe border, taking a frustrating two hours to queue to reach the one official behind a grill who would stamp our passports. There was a suggestion box, and we all thought of suggesting a larger building and more staff, but our comments might have also had some vitriolic additions to the basic thought, so none of us put pen to paper.

The area of present-day Zimbabwe has been the site of several organised states and kingdoms since the 11th century. British influence had been expanding in the area since the first colonists arrived in South Africa. In 1652, a century and a half after the discovery of the Cape Sea route, Jan van Riebeek established a victualling station at the Cape of Good Hope, in what would become Cape Town, on behalf of the Dutch East India Company. Some of the employees stayed after they completed their contracts, and more settlers arrived.

These forward-thinking entrepreneurs needed labour, so they imported slaves from Indonesia, Madagascar, and East Africa. When the First French Republic invaded the Low Countries, Britain occupied the colony from 1795 to 1803 to prevent it from coming under the control of the French. It was re-occupied in 1806 at the start of the Napoleonic Wars and ceded to the British at the end of the war.

Many of the Dutch settlers were unhappy about being under British control and moved out of the colony. They headed north and established new states such as Natal Orange Free State and Transvaal. However, British control spread north, and they fought the First Boer War (1880-1881) and ultimately included these territories into the British colony after the Second Boer War (1899-1902).

Meanwhile, the British South African Company, headed by Cecil Rhodes, ordered its Pioneer Column, financed by the company, to march into the area known today as Zimbabwe in 1890. He first demarcated the territory, ruled it over the next few years, and named it after himself, Rhodesia. He was an adventurer and wanted to expand the British Empire. At the time, all British possessions on a map were coloured red, and he had an ambition to create a wide band of red all the way up the continent, from the Cape to Cairo.

In 1922, the area was offered the opportunity to become part of South Africa, but the electorate rejected it, and in 1923, it became the self-governing British colony of Southern Rhodesia (to differentiate it from Northern Rhodesia, present-day Zambia). After the end of the Second World War, many former colonies were becoming independent. In an effort to delay the transition to majority black rule in 1965, the conservative white minority government made a unilateral declaration of independence (referred to as UDI) and named the country Rhodesia.

The country suffered international isolation and a 15-year guerrilla war against black nationalist forces in Rhodesia's Bush War. There was ZAPU, the Zimbabwe African People's Union led by Joshua Nkomo and ZANU, Zimbabwe African National Union, which split in 1975 into wings loyal to Robert Mugabe and Ndabaningi Sithole, later respectively called ZANU-PF and ZANU-Ndonga.

A peace agreement was agreed in April 1980, and the country was renamed Zimbabwe. Robert Mugabe won the elections, became Prime Minister of Zimbabwe in 1980, and ended white minority rule. He became President of Zimbabwe in 1987 and served until his resignation in 2017 to become one of the longest-serving heads of state in Africa. In 2017, ZANU-PF sacked Robert Mugabe as party leader and appointed former Vice President Emmerson Mnangagwa in his place, and Robert Mugabe resigned.

Under Mugabe's authoritarian regime, the state's security apparatus dominated the country and was responsible for widespread human rights violations. Mugabe maintained the revolutionary socialist rhetoric of the Cold War era, blaming Zimbabwe's economic woes on conspiring with Western capitalist countries in long speeches at mass rallies for which he is renowned. Contemporary African political leaders were reluctant to criticise Mugabe, who was buoyed by his anti-imperialist stance, though Archbishop Desmond Tutu called him "a cartoon figure of an archetypal African dictator". The country has been in economic decline since the 1990s, experiencing several economic crashes and hyperinflation along the way.

Zimbabwe's participation in the war in the Democratic Republic of the Congo from 1998 to 2002 set the stage for this deterioration by draining the country of hundreds of millions of dollars. Hyperinflation in Zimbabwe was a major problem from 2003 to 2009 destroying people's savings and making the currency worthless. The local currency was suspended in 2009, and all government transactions were to be in USD. Up to 2014, other foreign currencies were legal, with eight legal currencies circulating in the country: the US dollar, South African rand, Botswana pula, British pound sterling, Australian dollar, Chinese yuan, Indian rupee, and Japanese yen.

The country has reserves of metallurgical-grade chromite and other deposits such as coal, asbestos, copper, nickel, gold, platinum, diamonds, and iron ore, so it should be a rich country. However, corruption at government levels, poor management, and the pocketing of profits or theft of production by the ruling elite have damaged output. Gold output in 1998 was 27 tons but by 2007, it had fallen to just 7 tons. Even by 2015, it had only crept back to 18 tons, but it is suspected that gold production nationally is higher. Some small producers sell production into the black market for USD rather than the local currency bond notes that are allegedly worth the same as a dollar but are produced by the local Central Bank. The Marange diamond fields, discovered in 2006, are thought to be among the richest in the world, but mismanagement and corruption have seen a lot of production syphoned off to private bank accounts.

Meanwhile, the government's land reform seized and forcibly redistributed most of the country's white-owned, commercial farms. The new occupants included not just poor, landless black citizens but several prominent members of the ruling ZANU-PF administration. This, it is suggested, shows that they were getting rich on government policies and is proof of corruption. The new owners and occupants were usually inept, inexperienced, or uninterested in farming or doing any hard work, but just wanted to own large estates. The white-owned farms were labour intensive, providing jobs for hard working agricultural labourers, and the traditional white management of the farms was highly efficient.

Short-term gains for the new owners were achieved by selling the land or equipment. The lack of agricultural expertise triggered severe export losses and negatively affected market confidence. Commercial farmland became fallow or was being utilised by rural communities practicing subsistence farming. Production of staple foodstuffs, such as maize, has recovered, but internationally traded commodities such as cotton, sugar, tobacco, fruit, peanuts, and coffee for export have suffered steep falls. The University of Zimbabwe estimated in 2008 that between 2000 and 2007, agricultural production decreased by 51%, resulting in a loss of rural agricultural jobs, and production of tobacco, Zimbabwe's main and valuable export crop, producing nearly 25% of exports by value, decreased by 79% from 2000 to 2008.

State enterprises are heavily subsidised whilst taxes and tariffs are high. State regulation is costly for companies, and starting a business is slow and expensive. The labour market is highly regulated, so hiring a worker is cumbersome and firing a worker is difficult. By 2008, unemployment had risen to 94% and continued to rise. There are other structural issues, such as the perceived lack of a free press.

Energy production is a crucial area of the economy. The Kariba Dam, part owned by Zambia, provides large quantities of hydroelectric power. The Kariba Dam is downstream of Victoria Falls and is a double curvature concrete arch dam in the Kariba Gorge of the Zambezi River basin between Zambia and Zimbabwe. The dam stands 128 metres tall and 579 metres long. The dam forms Lake Kariba, which extends for 280 kilometres upstream.

The Kariba Dam supplies 1,626 megawatts of power. Zambia and Zimbabwe both have power houses on their sides of the river, and both power houses have been upgraded in recent years to increase output. In 2013, it was announced by Zimbabwe's Finance Minister, Patrick Chinamasa, that capacity at the Zimbabwean (South) Kariba hydropower station would be increased by 300 megawatts.

The cost of upgrading the facility has been supported by a loan from China at a cost of USD 533m. The deal is a clear example of Zimbabwe's "Look East" policy, which was adopted after falling out with Western powers. Construction on the Kariba South expansion began in mid-2014 and was completed ahead of schedule in 2018.

Another major power provider since 1983 is the large Hwange Thermal Power Station adjacent to the Hwange coal field, which has been reliably generating large amounts of power for decades. The Hwange coal mine lies 100 kilometres southeast of Victoria Falls and, at current extraction levels, had sufficient coal reserves for a thousand years. The coal field was discovered in 1895 by Frederick Russell Burnham. Coal has been mined here ever since, and the coal mining company was quoted on the London Stock Exchange, although the town and the mine were known as Wankie until 1982. There was a massive disaster here in June 1972, when the deadliest mining disaster in the country's history took place. An underground explosion occurred in Wankie No 2 Colliery, and 427 miners lost their lives.

Coal from here is transported by the mining railway to Thomson Junction, where it is handed over to the National Railways of Zimbabwe (NRZ) for onward transportation. In 2010, Botswana, Zimbabwe, and Mozambique signed an agreement to develop a railway for the export of coal to Technobanine Point near Maputo, more than 1,400 kilometres to the southeast.

However, total generation capacity does not meet the demand, leading to rolling blackouts. The Hwange station is not capable of using its full designed capacity due to old age and poor maintenance. In 2006, crumbling infrastructure and a lack of spare parts for both the power stations and the coal mining industry led to Zimbabwe importing 40% of its power from all of its neighbours.

Between 2000 and 2007, the national economy contracted by as much as 40%, whilst inflation skyrocketed to over 66,000% per annum. There were persistent shortages of hard currency, fuel, medicine, and food. Gross domestic product per capita plummeted by over 40% with agricultural output dropping by 51% and industrial production dropping by 47%.

However, the situation in Victoria Falls bears no witness to the poor economic outlook for the rest of the country, as the economy here is based on the thousands of tourists that visit the area every year. It was just a short drive to Victoria Falls from the border. Locals call it Mosi-oa-Tunya, meaning The Smoke That Thunders, and for many tourists, this is the highlight of their African safari. Seen from the main road coming from the border, in the bush 20 kilometres away, a cloud of mist and spray can be seen rising above the jungle against the blue sky. The Zambesi is over a kilometre wide, and more than five million cubic metres of water plunge over the edge every minute.

David Livingstone, a Scottish missionary and explorer, was the first European to discover the waterfall in 1855. He named them Victoria Falls in honour of Queen Victoria. On the Zambian side of the river is a national park named Mosi-oa-Tunya in the indigenous Lozi language, but the park on the Zimbabwean side and the town are both named Victoria Falls.

As you get closer, a low rumble, like thunder, can be heard. But there is also a lot of other noise. There are railways and marshalling yards, and there is a constant coming and going of planes and helicopters flying tourists over the falls, as well as the usual urban noises of traffic and jungle noises. However, we were not going to the falls straight away but stopped at a travel agency to book up our preferred choice of activities.

Victoria Falls is an adrenaline centre with a lot of options. There are helicopters, small planes, and microlight options to see the falls. There is bungee jumping from the bridge over the gorge just downstream from the falls or from the cliff overlooking the falls. There is trekking, horse riding, go-karting, and a host of other activities to choose from, but due to the high water levels, there were no rafting options as it was considered too dangerous.

We chose our preference for activities and then made our way to the camp site to set up the kitchen and our tents and relax for the rest of the afternoon. Some people went for a scenic helicopter or plane ride over the falls, and it seemed that there was a constant coming and going of small aircraft in the skies as I sat in camp.

That evening, most of us went to Bomas. This is a well-known restaurant for an 'all you can eat' evening meal and a bar. It is renowned for its selection of game meats, and most of the animals that we had seen were on offer, plus, of course, the usual beef, lamb, and chicken options. The meat selection is great, but the fish selection is limited, and there is only salad for vegetarians and vegans.

I was waiting to order at the bar, but there was a coachload of loud and pushy Americans at the bar. They were pushing in, waving their fistfuls of dollars, and leaning over the bar, shouting, and ordering drinks irrespective of who was first at the bar. I lost patience and walked out, asking at reception whether there was another bar. No, it wasn't, but why was I asking? I explained how annoyed I was with the conduct of the other patrons and not getting served in order. She took me back to the bar and got one of the staff to serve me. Looking at the three deep press at the bar, I might not have another opportunity to get back to the bar and get served, and I hate queuing, so I ordered three drinks for myself.

The buffet section was excellent, and everything was cooked to perfection. I tried a small portion of most of the dishes, concentrating on the unusual dishes and meats. I concentrated on the savoury selection, but it seemed that those loud, pushy Americans who were at the bar earlier were concentrating on the traditional European style desserts, so I didn't have to queue up to fill up with another savoury dish again. After the meal had been served, although many people were still eating, there was a drumming demonstration, and those who were not going back to the dessert buffet for fourths and fifths, were all given a pair of bongos so that we could join in.

I had a great night's rest and was up early to start breakfast. We have cook group, but we would be here for several days, and it was an opportunity to relax and have a lie-in. Therefore, breakfast was scheduled for later than usual. I had volunteered to set up the kitchen the night before, as I was often the first one up anyway, and there would be several early risers who expected breakfast before they had sunrise flights across Victoria Falls or whatever other activity they had booked. However, I didn't cook any breakfast for myself; I set it all up for people to help themselves, then I walked over to the campsite's restaurant for a bit of luxury and ordered a full English breakfast.

I had an important personal job to do. I needed to be at the DHL office at midday to send my passport back to the Ethiopian Embassy in London to get a visa. Ethiopian visas can be obtained at the airport, but if you are crossing a land border, they need to be applied for in your home country. I also wanted to visit Victoria Falls from both the Zimbabwean and Zambian sides. Therefore, I needed to get over the border and back again before lunchtime.

Chapter 6
Overnight Train to Bulawayo

The White man is not indigenous to Africa. Africa is for Africans. Zimbabwe is for Zimbabweans.
Robert Mugabe

If you close your eyes to facts, you will learn through accidents.
Kenyan proverb

I walked towards the Zimbabwe-Zambia border and was harassed by the usual throngs of souvenir sellers, but not in the usual numbers as I was crossing early in the morning. I ignored them all, as I was on a mission. I crossed the border and walked over the bridge, which was a half road bridge just wide enough for one vehicle at a time, whilst the other half was made up of railway tracks connecting Zambia to Zimbabwe and ultimately to the coast. The central arch has a graceful parabolic curve over the gorge just below Victoria Falls.

The bridge was prefabricated in England by the Cleveland Bridge & Engineering Company, before being shipped to the Mozambique port of Beira and then transported up the newly constructed railway to Victoria Falls. It took just 14 months to construct and was completed in 1905.

The bridge links Zambia to Zimbabwe and, via multiple rail links, to ports in Mozambique and South Africa. Zambia's largest export is copper, and despite the railway, there were a lot of lorries loaded with copper ingots waiting at the border to get into Zimbabwe. It is disappointing that the eco-friendlier option of rail transport for heavy loads has been superseded by the cheaper and quicker but more carbon inefficient option of road transport.

From the bridge, there is a good view of the gorge, but looking upstream, there is only a glimpse of the falls. I walked up the far side and into the Zambian

National Park to view the falls. There was a lot of spray, which obscured the falls. There was high water, and the river was full. The extra water cascading over the lip of the falls made a lot of spray, and it was hard to see very much of it at all.

There is a pedestrian bridge connecting the bank to a headland overlooking the gorge. It is so close to the falls that it is constantly being showered with spray. People can buy a plastic poncho to keep them dry from eager street vendors. However, this is a wasteful use of plastic, and despite the cheap price, it probably gets used just once and then is thrown away or left in the bottom of a wardrobe when the tourists get home.

I came prepared with a plastic bag and swimming trunks. I stripped down, put everything into the bag, and carried my clothes and shoes to cross the 40-metre-long bridge. It is constantly wet and slippery, with algae growing all over it. I trusted my bare feet more than my shoes, but that little bit is the only bit where you get wet. It is like standing under a shower with the water turned on full. I saw all of the Zambian side of the falls before crossing back to Zimbabwe.

Then I went into the Zimbabwe National Park and viewed the falls from their side. It was more expensive, but you do get better views. However, you still get wet—not in a downpour, but there is a constant mist and occasional showers when the wind picks up and pushes some spray across the path.

I visited the DHL office to post off my passport. I am always wary of travelling without a passport, but I had a photocopy of it and my visa, so if there was any query, I had at least some proof of identity. I really dislike being in a foreign country without a passport, but the Ethiopian visa is only valid for three months, so I could not apply for it before I left my home country.

I had lunch at The River Brewing Co., a microbrewery that also served food. I tried several of their beers over lunch. Then I stopped off at the railway station to enquire about tourist trains that serve dinner. There were spaces, and it cost USD180. But the problem for me was that today was Wednesday and the trains only run on Tuesday and Friday, and I was leaving (by train as it happened) on Friday, so I was out of luck. Similar trains run from Zambia, which would have fit my itinerary, but I had already posted my passport. I regret that I did a little more research so that I could have had dinner on a train and seen some of the scenery, and I could have fitted in with the schedule and rearranged my options.

So instead, I looked around the marshalling yards and some of the trains and bits of trains. There were several locomotives shunting wagons, so I watched for a while. This is a major shunting station where trains are re-configured depending on their final destination. After a while, I had had enough of watching shunting engines go back and forth, and I headed back to camp.

The option that I had booked when I first arrived in Victoria Falls was to go for a ride on a horse. I was picked up at 6.30am and taken by Joseph to the Zambesi Horse Safaris stables just a mile down the road from the camp. I was wearing shorts and a tee shirt due to the heat, even at that early hour of the morning, but I had my riding equipment in a bag. I was greeted by the owner, Alison, whose first comment after greeting me was whether I had been told what to wear.

I reassured her that I knew what to wear and changed into long trousers and a long-sleeved shirt. I put on some chaps and adjusted a helmet to fit comfortably. Then I was introduced to my two guides, named Senior and Lot leading just myself. Alison checked on my riding ability and checked that I had riding boots and a helmet that fit and that they were comfortable. I had my safety lecture, but what was different about this briefing was that it was made absolutely clear that I was to always stay behind the lead guide and always be behind him when viewing the game, and my back would be protected by Lot, who would always be at the back.

There are lots of thorn trees and acacia with wicked spikes, so you must get as low as possible on the horse's back and head, butt them with your helmet. I was told to make no noise unless your guide starts making a lot of noise, and then be as loud as you can. It is a precaution to discourage lions if you confront one. An arm waved in a circle, meant to turn around and walk away. The guide will have seen something, and you need to retreat. Always hold the reins, and don't get off your horse. There was more to remember, and I don't remember all the details, but it was all to do with how to react to the wildlife that we might encounter. My only question was about snakes and whether the horses are used to them. Some horses are afraid of snakes and anything that resembles them, such as hosepipes and ropes, but I was assured that these horses are used to snakes. But it was a question I would always ask so that I was prepared and could manage my mount if it reared.

Seniors then led the way out of the stables carrying a large air horn, which was to be used in the case of lions. Within minutes, we saw and skirted about two large elephants. Then we saw several kudus, and they darted around us as if unsure what to do or which direction to go. Being on horseback, we didn't appear to be human, so we could get very close without causing concern.

The next wildlife encounter was a Cape buffalo. This is one of the Big Five, as they have a short temper and attitude, can be unpredictable, and can charge, gore or trample you. They didn't see us as people but just watched us as we went past just five metres away, which is a lot closer than you would ever get to them if you were on foot. We rode through the jungle dodging thorn trees, but inevitably I got scratched despite the long sleeves, but I covered my eyes with one hand when I couldn't get any lower on the horse's back.

There were impalas, more kudu, and the tracks of zebras, lions, giraffes, and elephants. There were also tracks of crocodiles. They often move on land to get to the next waterhole, but only at night, which is another reason why Africans traditionally don't go out after dusk. Although there were no waterholes nearby, they move at night and may rest in shade during the day if they have not gotten to the next waterhole. The foot marks were indistinct, but there was a distinct groove in the sand where it had dragged its tail through the soil.

We saw a family of warthogs and stopped to let them cross the trail ahead of us, rummaging as they went. There were numerous aardvark holes that were pointed out, but we saw none of the animals themselves. But there were plenty of holes, and some are used by other slow-moving animals if there is a forest fire. They are also temporary homes for snakes, warthogs, porcupines, and aardvarks in emergencies, so you never know what may be down there, and you certainly don't put a hand in.

I was starting to become an expert in droppings, large football-sized balls of coarse fibres were elephants. Large black pellets were aardvarks, or could be giraffes, so check for prints. Small piles of pellets were kudu, and so on. Hyena droppings are often white from the amount of calcium they have ingested when crunching and swallowing bones.

Several birds were pointed out, but most flew off before I got a good look at them. But the white-backed vultures were more accommodating, standing at the top of a tall dead tree, so you had an opportunity to get a good photo. There were piles of feathers from two guinea fowl who didn't escape some predator. The head of Cape buffalo had been picked clean but had no other bones, not even the pelvis, just the skull and horns that had been left to roast in the sun.

We walked the horses to a nearby stream, which was also a waterhole, looking for crocodiles, but we found none. I was a bit apprehensive about splashing through the water, but the guides and horses didn't seem perturbed. But we did find a large herd of Cape buffalo on the far side of the river. They are active in the morning and evening, but during the heat of the day, they tend to stand or lie in the shade and chew the cud. We had to make several diversions to get past them safely.

And we made another diversion to get around some elephants hiding in some deep bush. More warthogs came past us. We stopped under a baobab tree and tried some of its fruit, which is edible. The fruit can be squeezed to make juice, and you can add sugar and milk to make it more palatable. It is a favoured drink locally, but the flavour was not to my palate. We got back to the stables, and our horses were led away, I had an opportunity to take some refreshments, followed by a shower and a chance to change into cooler shorts and a T-shirt. I was taken by car by Senior back to the campsite, and I said farewell.

That afternoon, Gareth was celebrating his birthday at the bar in Backpackers. I bought him a drink, but it was too noisy for me, with a lot of people having started toasting his health several hours before I arrived. I made my way into town to do some shopping and have a look around for a couple of hours.

We packed our overnight bags and walked into town. We were taking the overnight train from Victoria Falls to Bulawayo, all of us except Gareth, who would be driving the truck from Victoria Falls to our campsite in Bulawayo. We waited at the station for the train to pull in. It seemed to be quite a popular service, with almost as many tourists as Zimbabweans. I was getting excited, as I love travelling by train. It was an opportunity to look at the scenery as the train chugs along, and you can stretch your legs and walk about at the same time.

After waiting for what seemed like a long while, the train pulled into the station. It was pulled from three diesel-electric locomotives. I had half expected to see a steam engine, but at least they were early. We walked along the platform to find our carriage and our compartments. It was a mixed train of several passenger carriages and some coal trucks.

The coaches had been built in 1958 for Rhodesian Railways, and their logo, a double capital R with the first R reversed, was on all the mirrors and windows in the doors. There are several standards of train, luxury tourist class, 1st, 2^{nd,} and 3rd. We were on a second-class train, but we had been warned to expect primitive conditions. But for me, whatever the conditions, the views and experience of looking out the window and watching the world go by more than make up for any lack of first-class facilities.

The downside was that we would be travelling overnight, and therefore I would miss some of the scenery, which has always been my primary purpose for taking a train. The conditions were basic, just as promised. The toilet flushed straight out onto the tracks. There were no locks on the toilet doors. The basin was chipped, tired, and worn and was probably the original fitting. And there was no water in the taps. You had to provide your own toilet paper, soap, and water. The seats were hard and covered in worn plastic leather, which looks similar to fabric that doubled as a berth during the night. The floors had been swept, but they had the look of six decades of dirty boots having walked across them. Some of the outer train doors didn't shut probably, and you had to be careful as you walked along the train to hold on when you passed one of the broken doors so as not to fall out.

The sun soon set, and I lost the view out of the windows. There were several stops throughout the night, and people got off or got on and walked along the train to find their seats. There was a restaurant car, but they only had dried sandwiches with the corners turned up. They had no cold drinks, just warm beer, or coca cola. We saw the sun rise over the jungle, and we had breakfast of fruit, yoghurt, and muffins that Kim had brought with her for the group.

Then we passed a luxury tourist train. It was a short section of double track. They were stationary, and we rolled past slowly, giving us ample opportunity to goggle through the windows. The carriages were modern and clean. There were deeply upholstered armchairs, air conditioning, wood panelling, space between tables in the dining car, menus, waitress service, hot coffee and cold fruit juices, flowers on the tables, carpets on the floor, and I was instantly jealous, but only for a moment. After all, the scenery was the same, and our tickets cost just USD 12 each (the locals pay a tenth of that on the third-class train), whereas their tickets would have cost a hundred times more.

We knew we were approaching Bulawayo as the jungle turned to fields, which in turn were ultimately swamped by the urban fringe. We stopped next to some marshalling yards, and the coal trucks on our train were unhooked and pulled away by another locomotive.

Bulawayo is the second-largest city in Zimbabwe, with an estimated population of 1.2 million. The city was founded by the Ndebele king, Lobengula, in the 1840s. There was a civil war in progress at the time, and he used the

Ndebele word KoBulawayo, meaning "a place where he is being killed" to name the place, and his generals asked, "who is being killed, king?" and he replied, "it's me, the king, who is being killed."

The city is nicknamed the "City of Kings" and also "kontuthu ziyathunqa"—a Ndebele phrase for "smoke arising". This name arose from the city's historically large industrial base and specifically draws from the large cooling towers of the coal powered electricity generating plant situated in the city centre that once used to billow steam and smoke over the city and the industrial centre of Zimbabwe. The city is the hub of the country's rail network, with the National Railways of Zimbabwe headquartered here because of its strategic position on major railway lines providing links to Botswana, Zambia, Mozambique, and South Africa.

Our train pulled into the terminus at Bulawayo station. The three locomotives were disconnected and driven away. I had hoped for a large Victorian style station, but it was a functional two-storey red brick and white limestone affair, and whilst it was interesting, it was not the grand façade that I had hoped to see.

We were met by our hosts, Andy, and Lynette, plus Christine, who runs Burke's Paradise, which was where we were going to stay for a few days. We drove through the city, passing several derelict and abandoned industrial sites, and out of town to a prosperous neighbourhood of large houses set in equally large gardens, often surrounded by discreet security fences. We set up our tents next to the swimming pool area, whilst some of the group got upgrades to really nice rooms with soft beds and ensuite facilities. I roughed it up in a tent for the time that we were in Bulawayo, having spent more than was in my budget in Victoria Falls, and I was keen to get back on budget.

Chapter 7
Chimanimani National Park

The magician and the politician have much in common; they both have to draw our attention away from what they are doing.
Ben Okri

Do not fight a lion if you are not a lion yourself.
African proverb

I walked to the nearest shop. It was along the main road into the city centre, and I walked along with one eye over my shoulder. The most popular means of getting around the city is by taxi bus. These are privately operated minivans that follow a set route, and you just stand at the edge of the road and flag one down when it appears. The cost is negligible, but these minivans coming past had a long route and were nearing their final destination. They were often full when they came past.

The locals are very friendly, and even if there are no seats, they will squash up and make space. However, I wanted a pleasurable ride and not to be squashed, so I let several full minivans go past. I reached the local shops before a minivan with a spare seat came past. I bought a few things for the barbecue that evening and walked back to Burke's Paradise.

Our next stop was the Matobo National Park. It was set up in 1926 as Rhodes Matopos National Park with a bequest from Cecil Rhodes and covers over 3,100 square kilometres. The current name, Matobo, reflects the correct vernacular pronunciation of the name for the area. The name means 'bald head' which is what some of the rocks that stand above ground level resemble. The park includes the Matobo Hills, which were designated as a UNESCO World Heritage

Site in 2003. The area includes a number of distinctive rock formations rising above the granite shield that covers much of Zimbabwe.

It is an area of high botanic diversity, with over 200 species of tree, recorded in the national park, including the mountain acacia, wild pear, and paperbark tree. There are also many aloes, wild herbs, and over 100 grass species. It is claimed that the park has the world's densest population of leopards, due to the abundance of hyrax, which make up 50% of their diet. There are also large populations of hyenas, hippopotamus, giraffes, zebras, wildebeests, and ostriches.

The park has white rhinoceros, which were introduced in the 1960's, from Kwa-Zulu Natal, and black rhinos, introduced from the Zambezi Valley in the 1990's. It has been designated as an Intensive Protection Zone for the two species, and pairs of armed rangers follow each animal for their protection.

No sooner than we were inside, we stopped, and our guides, Lynette and Andy, a former game hunter turned eco tourist guide, pointed out a white rhino. We got out of the 4x4 and quietly walked over in a single file. The animal looked at us a few times and then turned and walked away, so we left it in peace and moved on.

We came across an armed ranger with an AK47 standing in the shade beside the road. She directed us to her colleague in the bush, who was watching several rhinoceros. She spent the day with her colleague, following and guarding the rhinos. The rhinos are subject to poaching for meat and for their horns. There is a belief that the powdered horn is an aphrodisiac. Part of this belief stems from the fact that rhinoceros' sex is not quick, but mating can take 45 minutes. Since the economic crisis, jobs are scarce, and there is 96% unemployment. People are returning to their villages to grow subsistence crops and go hunting for extra protein or for horns to sell. Everyone knows someone who can trade ivory or rhinoceros' horn.

We walked with the rhinoceros, a mother with two offspring, one large and one small, but the largest one was not yet ready to be independent and leave his mother. They just browsed, and we could get within five metres. It was absolutely exhilarating.

We moved on to a picnic spot and had some cold pasta and salad in the shade of some trees. We crossed the Malene dam, and watched the crocodiles. Nearby is a walk through the bush to some caves high up on the side of one of the hills. Inside are a number of cave paintings, made by the local San people and estimated to be up to 13,000 years old. We walked to the top of the hill for the marvellous views across the kopjes.

We moved on to another hill where Cecil Rhodes grave is situated on top of the hill. Not only is Cecil Rhodes buried here, but Sir Leander Starr Jameson is also buried here, best known for his failed attempt at leading a private army to invade Transvaal in a bid to topple the Boer government led by Paul Kruger, known as the Jameson Raid.

On another part of the hill stands the Allan Wilson Memorial, which commemorates the leader of the Shangani Patrol during the First Matabele War, and his bravery and death fighting overwhelming odds made him a hero. After looking around the graves and memorials, we sat on the top of the hill and watched the lizards and elephant shrews, waiting for the sunset before returning to Bulawayo.

The first stop after leaving Burke's Paradise was the Bulawayo Railway Museum, located in some former sidings of the vast marshalling yards in Bulawayo. There are all sorts of locomotives and carriages on display, with the oldest exhibits dating back to 1897. Cecil Rhodes had his own coach, which is on display in the museum. It is the first locomotive to cross the Victoria Falls railway bridge, which was completed in 1905.

Then we had a two-hour drive to head northeast to Antelope Park near the town of Gweru for more activities and to see lions. It is a 1,200-hectare reserve and the base of ALERT, the African Lion Environment Research Trust, for research, rehabilitation, and a programme that focuses on the release of animals back into the wild. There is a range of accommodation from camping to individual rooms to upmarket lodges for hire. It was James' birthday, and he decided to upgrade straight away to a cabin overlooking a river.

There were all sorts of activities available, and we would be here for several days, so there was plenty of opportunity to indulge yourself in several. They were walking with lions, interacting with elephants, canoeing, horse riding and horse lessons, snake handling, carriage rides, lion feeding, and game drives. There was so much on offer that some of us were spoilt for choice.

I went walking with lions and later saw the lion feeding. After walking with cheetahs a few weeks earlier, this was a bit of a non-event for me. If it was your first walk with wild predators, it would have been exciting, but my cheetah experience was still so recent that lions were not that much of a novelty. I went for a ride as well, but I like to ride all day, so this was just a two-hour walk around some local tracks. The horses probably did this every day and didn't show much spirit. We were also a group of mixed riding abilities, and the guide didn't want anybody to leave the group for a trot, canter, or gallop or for people to be out of their depth. Hence, it was just a walk around some of the enclosures to see lions, zebras, and giraffes from the back of a horse.

I went for a walk across the bridge over the river to the far side of the resort. There were more lodges and accommodations, but these were closed and out of use as it was the low season for tourism. I went back to the central facilities and relaxed in the bar, overlooking the river. It was so relaxing and quiet that I fell asleep and had to be gently nudged awake for supper back at the camp site. Our meals were all self-catering and included in the camping option, but I did take one night out to go to the restaurant to have a taste of some of the local fish dishes.

It was also here that I received my first bond notes. This was currency that circulated in Zimbabwe, printed by the government, which had the same value as the USD but was not currency accepted outside Zimbabwe and could not be exchanged for any foreign currency. The two- and five-dollar notes were allegedly backed by actual American dollars held by the Central Bank. However, given the dire experience of the former local currency and hyperinflation, there is not a lot of faith placed in these bond notes. They are legal tender, so it is difficult to refuse them, but I would always ask for my change in USD dollars. Whenever I got them and didn't get real USD's, I would spend them as fast as possible.

We left Antelope Park and drove through Masvingo, formerly called Fort Victoria until 1982, allegedly the oldest colonial settlement in present-day Zimbabwe and the site of the first cricket match in the country in 1890. From there, we went on to the most famous tourist attraction nearby, the city of Great Zimbabwe.

Great Zimbabwe was a mediaeval city and is recognised as a World Heritage Site by UNESCO. It was the capital of the Kingdom of Zimbabwe, with construction of the city starting in the 11th century, and the city was occupied until the 15th century. The buildings were erected by the ancestral Shona. The stone city spans an area of over 700 hectares, which, at its peak, could have housed up to 18,000 people. The great granite blocks that make up the city were skilfully put together by stone masons, but they used no mortar or cement.

The kingdom covered an area of present-day Zimbabwe and stretched into Botswana and South Africa. It was a large empire that traded goods widely, especially with coastal tribes and Arab merchants who sailed down the coast and who had major trading centres such as Dar es Salaam.

The ruins at Great Zimbabwe are some of the oldest and largest structures located in Southern Africa and are the second oldest after nearby Mapungubwe in South Africa. Its most formidable edifice, commonly referred to as the Great Enclosure, has walls reaching 11 metres and extending approximately 250 metres across, making it the largest ancient structure south of the Sahara Desert. Its growth was probably linked to several factors, such as the decline of neighbouring Mapungubwe from around 1300 due to climatic change and the greater availability of gold in the hinterland of Great Zimbabwe.

The ultimate abandonment of the site at around 1450 has been suggested to be due to a decline in trade compared to sites further north, the exhaustion of the gold mines, political instability, overpopulation, famine, and water shortages induced by climatic change. It is estimated that they exported an estimated 4,000 tons of alluvial gold from nearby rivers.

After our tour of the ancient city of Great Zimbabwe, it was too late to move on, so we camped in the grounds. The big disadvantage of camping here was that there were loads of monkeys around. They are both inquisitive and quick learners, and they know that they can get some easy pickings by raiding camps. Whilst the cook group prepared the evening meal, Stefano had armed himself and would throw firewood at the monkeys when they got too close. One monkey got lucky by going around the back of the truck out of sight to get near where the cook group was preparing supper. He then made a dash through the kitchen area, grabbing an avocado on his way and disappearing back into the trees.

In the morning, it was a pleasant drive to Lake Mutirikwe, which lies to the southeast of Masvingo and was formerly known as Lake Kyle. The lake was created in 1960 when a dam was built across the Mutirikwe River. The dam is 63 metres high and 309 metres long. The lake covers 90 square kilometres. The water is used for irrigation in the low veld to the southwest, where the major crop is sugar. The levels vary significantly due to seasonal rainfall and seasonal usage for crop irrigation.

Then it was a scenic and picturesque drive into the Eastern Highlands to camp outside Chimanimani National Park. There are many spectacular gorges and high peaks, the tallest being Mount Binga, rising to 2,436 metres. There are several streams cascading through the granite mountain formations, as well as numerous mountain springs. This is home to many wildlife species, such as eland, sable, bushbuck, blue duiker, klipspringer, and the occasional leopard, which I was still eager to see in the wild.

There are several hiking trails and an opportunity to visit the Bvumba Gardens. They are referred to as the "Mountains of the Mist", Bvumba being the Shona word for "mist", as often the early morning starts with a mist that clears by mid-morning. These gardens are popular with botany lovers. It is a garden endowed with indigenous orchids and ferns, with a network of footpaths that enable visitors to explore all the corners of the garden. There are opportunities to take a hike through the mountain wilderness area, hike to the nearby Bridal Veil Falls, or simply enjoy the stunning surroundings of this sleepy village and stroll through the village market.

It was noticeably colder in the highlands. There were upgrades available at Heaven Mountain Lodge, but I persevered with the tent option. The evening and night were cool, but I was comfortable in the tent. Some people went off for a long trek into the mountains to see a waterfall and stand on the border between Zimbabwe and Mozambique. Some went off to see the Bridal Veil Waterfalls, just five kilometres from the village of Chimanimani. I tried a few local bars, which were mainly dives, and in one of them, the bar staff worked behind a metal grill to separate them and keep them safe from the customers. It was daylight and seemed safe enough, but the need for the grill suggests that there is trouble here at night. I moved on to the Chimanimani Hotel. It was opened in 1952 based on a 1940's design and oozing art deco features, but regrettably underutilised.

The barman, a gentleman named Livingstone, spoke hopefully of elections in a few weeks' time to change the country. He pointed out that the country has plenty of land, it is fertile, there is water, there are minerals, and there is coal, so it should be a rich country, but there has been such corruption and squandering of national assets that the government has been unable to fund the health system or education for which the country was once held up as a leading light in Africa.

The country used to be called the breadbasket of the continent as it could grow so much food and sell it on world markets, but after land seizures, political interference, and a lack of stability, does not encourage people to stay and invest. This has robbed the country of its ability to be a hive of activity; exports have collapsed, jobs are scarce, and food, once cheap and abundant, is rising in price. Everyone I spoke to had the hope that the elections would transform the country, but they also spoke of corruption, and everyone was waiting to see what was behind the mountain, to use a local expression.

We moved on, taking the road via Matare to Harare. There was a railway line that ran alongside the road, and we saw a train, but just as we drew level and I raised my camera, there were trees that blocked the view, and then we overtook the train, and later the track pulled away from the road, and any chances of me getting a photo of the train vanished.

Harare was originally named Salisbury until 1982, when the city's name was changed on the second anniversary of Zimbabwe's independence. The city sits on a plateau at an elevation of 1,483 metres. The city was founded in 1890 by the Pioneer Column, a small military volunteer force of settlers organised by Cecil Rhodes and his British South Africa Company and named Fort Salisbury after the British Prime Minister Lord Salisbury. The settlement became a city in 1935. It is the country's largest city and hosts many of the country's largest company headquarters and their trading organisations.

In May 2005, the Zimbabwean government demolished several shanty towns and backyard cottages in Harare and the other cities in the country in Operation Murambatsvina, meaning "Drive Out Trash", a rather provocative name, but it was the one that was chosen. It was widely alleged that the true purpose of the campaign was to punish the urban poor for supporting the opposition Movement for Democratic Change, the opposition party, and to reduce the likelihood of mass action against the government. The Economist Intelligence Unit rated Harare as the world's worst city to live in out of the 140 surveyed in February 2011. The positive news is that it had risen to 137th out of 140 by August 2012.

We worked our way through the suburbs to find our Small World Lodge in Harare. It was a pleasant place, but the internet was poor, with so many users all wanting to use their phones and computers, and there are only a limited number of customers able to use it at any one time. We were camping on the grounds, but some upgrades to the dormitories were available. I put up the tent, but it wasn't in a good position as it was next to a path between the dormitories and the main building. There were also other guests staying there, but there was no other pitch available. I decided to upgrade to a hotel just down the road.

I wanted to check out the internet at the hotel before I booked a room, so I asked to try it out and use it to book a room. However, it was cheaper to book direct, so I thanked the receptionist, paid cash in US dollars, which was much appreciated by the receptionist, and made my way to my room. She was very helpful and was true to her word and my request, as she had given me a quiet room. It was on the top floor, at the far end of the corridor, and furthest away from the road and the painters who were decorating the other end of the building.

I walked into the centre of the city to find a computer shop. I wanted to load Microsoft 365 onto my Apple laptop, but it had to be compatible. There wasn't enough band width, so I couldn't do it myself. I walked around the city centre, trying several shops, but came away empty handed. That evening, the rest of the group was going to a barbecue. They left at 3pm and started early on the beers. I missed the departure as I was still walking around searching for various computer shops. Whilst the rest of the group was partying hard, I had a quiet evening meal of fish and rice in a local restaurant.

I got back to the lodge to take my tent down, ready for a midday departure. Apparently, it had been a great barbecue the night before, but most people were nursing a hangover. We loaded the truck and set off towards the Mozambique border. The truck was quiet, as people were catching up on their sleep. I was fine, as I had missed the party and had had an early night.

We headed towards the border and into some mountains. It was a very scenic route towards the Nyamapanda border crossing, and I had a bush camp nearby before crossing in the morning. We turned off the road and along a rough track over two streams to a clearing just off the track. We were just reversing into the clearing when a couple of locals and an ox cart walked along the road. They seemed happy to let us stay there, so we continued with setting up camp.

There were acacia trees everywhere with long spikes that caught on clothes and hair. We collected firewood, but after getting spiked several times by the long spines, we were more careful about how we picked up the pieces lying about. Nice pitches were rare, but I found a pitch on a path to nowhere. It wasn't flat, but I used a shovel to level out the site, so it wasn't such a steep slope, as I don't like sleeping with my feet higher than my head. I could have reoriented the tent, but that would mean a diversion through the trees to get back to the truck, and after being spiked collecting firewood, I wanted to avoid crashing through the thorn filled trees, especially in the dark.

We had a short drive to the border and arrived just behind two low-loaders. They were each carrying a tipper section of giant quarrying dump trucks. There was the width of a road and as high as a house. A brick pillar had been demolished to allow the trucks to pass. The first truck had driven through the gate, but it was trying to negotiate a path through some parked trucks, but there was insufficient room by just centimetres.

We walked through the border controls, got stamped out of Zimbabwe, and walked half a kilometre across no man's land to the Mozambique border. Gareth would have to wait with the truck until the low-loaders had negotiated the blockages. We filled in our visa forms and our immigration forms and handed over our passports and USD50, the cost of the visa. Then we had our fingerprints and photos taken. It took four hours to process all of us. The Low-loaders had come through Gareth had joined us, and we were all ready to go.

After several months of travelling through sophisticated and Westernised countries such as South Africa, Namibia, Botswana, and, to a degree, Zimbabwe, we were back in countryside, more akin to some of the West African nations with which I was familiar. What we hadn't seen in the last few countries and have taken for granted is now back in force: subsistence farming, no electricity, no mains water, no mains sewage, and poorly stocked corner stores. Bricks and concrete had been replaced with reed roofs and wattle walls, and a two-storey building was a novelty.

Many of the villages and houses in the country had stacks of timber and bags of charcoal neatly piled on the side of the road for sale. In fact, cutting down trees and creating charcoal for sale at the side of the road in Zimbabwe outside of licensed industrial processes is illegal. However, in Mozambique, it was one of the many ways that local people used the local resources to provide income to trade so that they could survive.

Between the first and fifth centuries, Bantu-speaking peoples migrated to present-day Mozambique from the north and west. Beginning in the 11th century, Arab, Persian, and Somali merchants began trading along the coast and established ports and settlements, contributing to the development of a distinct Swahili culture and language. The official language of the country is Portuguese, but half of the country's 29 million population speak it as a second language. Portuguese explorers had travelled down the west coast of Africa, passed the Cape of Good Hope, and were travelling up the east coast. Vasco da Gama visited here in 1498, and the Portuguese colonised the area.

There was a ten-year war of independence before Mozambique gained independence from Portugal in 1975, but after just two years, the country fell into a long and bitter civil war that didn't finish until 1992. In 1994, Mozambique held its first multiparty elections, and has since remained a relatively stable presidential republic, although it still faces a low intensity insurgency.

We stopped for fuel, either firewood or charcoal, and we found that the charcoal was cheap. There was litter at the sides of the road, blowing about into the fields and jungle. Most of it was plastic and would pollute the countryside for centuries, and it was being added to faster than nature could decompose it.

There were Africans walking along the edge of the road. Children were always walking along the roads to go to school, to come home, or just collecting water or wood for fuel. But now there were men or women with loads on their heads walking along the roads. Something else that I had noticed was that there were more bicycles here in Mozambique than any other country to date that I had visited in Africa. It was a sign of how poor they are, as people soon upgraded from a bicycle to a moped at the earliest opportunity.

We were also objects of fascination again. People waved and smiled as we drove through their villages. The children would stop whatever they were doing and shout and wave at us. Some even ran along the side of the road as they were shouting and waving. In the meantime, the women worked in the fields or in the yards, and the men sat under trees and talked.

Chapter 8
Bilharzia and Lake Malawi

Books and all forms of writing are a terror to those who want to suppress the truth.
Wole Soyinke

When two elephants fight, it is the grass that gets trampled.
Swahili proverb

I was surprised at how much land there was, but so little of it was cultivated. All the settlements seemed to have a few small fields next to the family hut, but there was jungle just beyond. It was all subsistence farming, with little or no surplus to sell. I recognise the need for game reserves and areas of natural beauty, but despite these limitations, there still seemed to be a lot of land that was left as nature intended but left unused by the local population to grow a surplus and trade it in the local market.

We drove through some hills and through Tete. It was nothing special, but there were a lot of houses spread over a large area. There were loads of people walking in both directions, everybody seemed to want to be somewhere else, walking through the rubbish at the side of the road. There were a lot of shacks selling drinks or sweets by the roadside, mostly jerry built. Some had crude hand-painted signs, as did some of the more substantial buildings, which were bars and restaurants, but few had proper signs. Most were hand-written, scrawled signs in whatever leftover paint the owner might have. And women are always carrying large loads on their heads.

That night was our first night in Mozambique, and we had a bush camp with a difference. We had been looking for a suitable site but couldn't find one, as every opportunity seemed to have a farmhouse next door or near the main road.

We passed an army post, and next door was a large, flat grassy area. The army post had a sign above the gate declaring it to be the barracks of the 3rd Battalion. But what we thought was just a flat area was their parade ground, but it was badly overgrown with grass and weeds. There were only a few soldiers on site, and after checking with the most senior officer, they let us use their parade ground to set up camp.

They let the girls use their toilet facilities, although all the girls reported back that it was dirty, there was no water in the taps, it smelled, and there were no doors. For the men, one of the soldiers pointed across the parade ground to the jungle on the far side. We thought that he meant that we were to do our business behind a tree, but after some of the more adventurous members of the group had explored the area, some distance into the jungle was a toilet block, but so heavily overgrown so as to be unusable. The parade ground was flat, but the downside was that it was difficult to bang in tent pegs or to dig a hole in the hard ground, so most of us waited until dark and disappeared into the jungle with a trowel.

Above the lockers in the back of the truck, just behind the cab, is a small, padded area the width of the truck and a couple of metres long. It is near the roof, so you can't sit there, but you can lie down. The roof above it is hinged and can be opened, but we don't drive with the top open as it is too much of a temptation to sit up and look out as it is dangerous with low hanging branches and telephone wires. This area is known as 'The Beach'. In the morning, as we were driving along, there were three people lying on the beach when suddenly Heather and Laura started clambering down, complaining loudly, and waving their hands in front of their noses. Noah, the other occupant of the beach, had let out a silent but deadly fart, which slowly filled up the small area and caused a sudden emergency evacuation of the area.

We crossed the border from Mozambique into Malawi. This part of Africa, now known as Malawi, was settled by migrating Bantu groups around the 10th century. David Livingstone discovered Lake Malawi in 1859, and later other Anglican and Presbyterian missionaries arrived to convert the population. African Lakes Corporation Co Ltd was set up in 1877 by Scottish businessmen to cooperate with Presbyterian missions. It operated its businesses in Africa on a commercial rather than philanthropic basis. Its businesses in the colonial era included water transport on the lakes and rivers of Central Africa, wholesale, and retail trading, and the operation of general stores.

A settlement was established in Blantyre in 1876, and a British consul took up residence here in 1883. In 1889, a British protectorate was proclaimed over the Shire Highlands, which was extended in 1891 to include the whole of present-day Malawi as the British Central Africa Protectorate. In 1907, the protectorate was renamed Nyasaland. In 1953, Nyasaland became a protectorate within the semi-independent Federation of Rhodesia and Nyasaland, similar to an area today comprising Zimbabwe, Zambia, and Malawi. The federation lasted for ten years. In 1964, Nyasaland became an independent country and was renamed Malawi. It became a totalitarian, one-party state under the presidency of Hastings Banda, who remained president until 1994. The country is among the world's least-developed countries. The economy is heavily based around agriculture, with a largely rural population and widespread overpopulation and unemployment.

After a relatively simple process of crossing into Malawi, we drove on to Lilongwe. Someone asked about the history of the city, and Chris was fast to explain that it was a Chinese admiral who had landed on the East African coast in the sixteenth century, explored inland, discovered this place, founded a city, and named it after himself. He said it so convincingly that some people believed him, but it was a complete fabrication, and only the most gullible fell for the ruse, and we all had a laugh.

We stopped at a supermarket, Shoprite, which is a chain that has shops seemingly throughout Africa. They are all large, modern, and stock everything that you might need. They have clean toilets and a selection of salads and cooked food that you can take away. I was cooking again with Chris and Noodles. But we were also on a budget, and whilst the supermarket had a good selection of foodstuffs, we opted to use the local fruit and vegetable market so that our budget stretched further.

We walked down the road into the market. We were mobbed from the first moment we appeared. Traders left their stalls and surrounded us. Their hands were full of produce that they wanted us to buy. Even though we each said no to bananas, the next trader would hold up a bunch and ask if we wanted bananas. And beyond the traders, there were inquisitive locals who wanted to see what was going on, so wherever we went, we were always surrounded.

There was also some antagonism amongst the traders, as each claimed that we were their customers, and there was some shouting and shoving. Traders were asking us what we wanted, and they would run away and return moments later, thrusting their produce under our noses. I found it all very intimidating and stressful. I was holding the bags, so I slipped towards the outer ring of the crowd and would dart in once Chris or Noodles made a purchase.

Noodles negotiated lower prices, but Chris took the prize as he was a marvellous market shopper and good at bartering. He negotiated hard and even got some of the traders to compete to get a trade, saving us more money. But we were also on a time limit, so we had to go back to the supermarket to get things that we needed that we couldn't find in the market.

As we shopped at Shoprite, we compared some of the prices. The eggs were cheaper in the supermarket, so we hadn't bargained hard enough for those, and we had to carry them carefully around the market as we did our shopping. Perhaps we should have bought them last to save any bangs that might have cracked the shells. But most of the fruit and vegetables were cheaper, and our pineapples from the market were 40% cheaper than from the supermarket. We were pleased with the overall accounting result, but I would be dreading the next Cook Group Shop if we were to be the centre of a rugby scrum.

We drove into the suburbs and stopped at the Mutayu Campsite. Here we met up with our sister truck, driven by Paul, whom I had first met in South America, so we could reminisce about old times. That evening at 5.30pm, the drivers and guides of the two trucks invited everyone for drinks and canapes for a 'get to know you' party. We also nosed about each other's trucks. Both vehicles were made the same but had been converted to overlanding trucks at different times and, inevitably, to different designs. Paul's truck also had fewer passengers, so there was sparer space, so it was much easier to keep tidy. In comparison, our truck looked cramped and untidy.

I was one of the first up in the morning to set up the kitchen and cook breakfast. For a change, we would be cooking a frittata, or our version of a Spanish omelette, basically finely chopped vegetables and eggs. It took a bit of preparation, and people were also up early, expecting hot drinks and something to eat. We were on time, but it is stressful to be watched by a lot of hungry overlanders expecting to be fed.

The only trouble was that halfway through breakfast, it started to rain. People who had had breakfast retreated to the truck. Thus, those who were yet to eat breakfast dashed across to the table, grabbed whatever was within reach, and also retreated to the truck. It is the cook group's responsibility to clear away the kitchen, and it is not their sole job. As we are a little, friendly community, normally people usually help each other out, which is all part of the fun of overlanding. But it was raining. Some people not in the cook group helped out to clear everything away, but there were some people like Noah and Kenny who just cowered in the truck out of the rain and left all the jobs to others.

Everything was packed away, and some of us were wet through. As the last of the cook group and our stalwart helpers climbed onto the truck, we dripped water. Also, in the back of the truck, with the windows shut against the rain, there was plenty of body heat, and we started steaming as the water evaporated off our wet clothes and misted up the windows.

Later in the day, it had stopped raining, so we were able to have the windows open to enjoy the view. It was a pleasant drive through rolling hills and mountains as we moved on from Lilongwe to Lake Malawi on a road that ran parallel to the lake shore. There were times that we couldn't see the lake, but every now and again we caught glimpses of it. Despite the distance, which wasn't that far, we made good time over the poor roads, and we arrived at Kande Beach in the late afternoon.

We were to have some communal fun games, but the roads had not been as good as expected, so not all the preparations had been completed as we drove along. Therefore, we postponed them until another time. The campsite overlooks Lake Malawi. It is Africa's third largest lake and the seventh largest in the world, and it makes up nearly a third of the country. It is at the end of the Great Rift Valley that stretches from here northwards through Africa to Ethiopia, then up the Red Sea, then carries on to the Dead Sea on the borders of Israel and Jordan, up the Bekaa Valley in Lebanon, Syria, and ends in Turkey. This is where two tectonic plates are pulled apart.

Soon we gathered around some tables under an open sided palm frond roofed shed with a drink. We cooked some hotdogs over a barbecue and played beer ping pong. Aficionados do not call ping pong anything other than table tennis, but the game we were playing ought to have a better name. Players have a table tennis table with some cups set up at one end, and the players have to bat a ball into one of the cups at the other end of the table. Simple in theory, but after a few drinks, the eye-to-hand coordination fails, and it can degenerate into a raucous party as everybody thinks that they can still play the game well. It was a bit unfair, as Zac is a great sportsman, and despite the rum punch and the lateness of the hour, he could still win most of the games.

We had a couple of nights here, so there was a whole day to fill. I walked up to the local village. Outside the gates to Kande Beach are a host of souvenir sellers that you can't avoid. They mostly had the same items on sale, some handcrafted locally: statues, face masks, traditional clothes, spears, and all sorts of other items. If you went out on foot, you would be mobbed, and it was no better on the way back.

There were all sorts of activities available, such as horse riding, a village walk, a trek into the hills, and the Kaningina Forest Reserve, and despite the bilharzia, there were plenty of water-based activities such as diving, snorkelling, paddle boarding, or just plain swimming in the lake.

Bilharzia, also known as schistosomiasis and snail fever, is a disease caused by parasitic flatworms called schistosomes found in Africa, Asia, and South America. The parasites live in freshwater snails and escape into the water to infect them. The urinary tract or the intestines may be infected. Symptoms include abdominal pain, diarrhoea, bloody stools, or blood in the urine. Those who have been infected for a long time may experience liver damage, kidney failure, infertility, or bladder cancer. In children, it may cause poor growth and learning difficulties.

Bilharzia is the second most economically damaging disease in the tropics after malaria. About 250 million people are affected, and between 4,400 and 200,000 die of it every year. The good news is that it is treatable, and the tablets are readily available from pharmacies. This is an easy solution for us in the wealthy West, but not for poor farmers in remote areas. This was just another reason why Africa was not on my bucket list. It has a host of deadly diseases that are unpleasant and can kill you.

There are insects that bite you, animals that kill and eat you, it is unpleasantly hot at times, and there is political instability with corruption, poverty, demonstrations, and civil unrest. I was still here, travelling through Africa. I had spent three months in Asia with a couple, Malcolm, and Grace, who had spent three years in Africa and had told so many anecdotes and stories about the continent that I was finally persuaded to go. And I still went for a swim, but I also went to the pharmacy in the next big town to get some medicine just in case.

The main road north of Kande Beach runs along the shoreline. I was looking forward to seeing more of the lake, but there were only a few views of the lake. Going further north, there are hills and mountains with deep valleys. It was a very scenic view as the road snaked its way through some spectacular scenery, but there were often trees or hills between us and the lake. There were some steep slopes, and the truck struggled in bottom gear to get to the top with views from our vantage point high above the lake. Then there was a steady descent.

We passed Livingstonia. The town was founded in 1894 by Free Church of Scotland missionaries. Their first mission was established in 1875 at Cape Maclear, on a peninsular at the southern end of Lake Malawi. The mission was linked with the Africa Lakes Corporation, so the mission concentrated on the spiritual needs of the population and Africa Lakes concentrated on the physical needs of transport and trade.

By 1881, Cape Maclear had proved extremely malarial, and the mission moved north to Bandawe, about two thirds up Lake Malawi, not far from Kande Beach. The site also proved unhealthy, and the Livingstonia Mission moved once again to higher ground between Lake Malawi and the Nyika Plateau, another 150 kilometres further north. This new site proved highly successful because this latest location for Livingstonia is located in the cooler mountains and therefore not prone to mosquitoes carrying malaria.

The mission station gradually developed into a small town. The original houses in Livingstonia are characteristic in that they are mostly constructed with red bricks. The leading missionary for the past 52 years. He established the best school for the whole region. There is a small museum about the history of Livingstonia, and inexpensive accommodation is available for travellers at the Stone House, the original house of Dr Robert Laws.

We were not staying in Livingstonia but a few kilometres up the coast at the Chitimba Campsite for another couple of days on the beach, a popular place for overlanding trucks to stop. There were various activity options, such as horse riding, plenty of trekking options, including some waterfalls at Manchewe Falls, and more water-based activities.

I would have liked to do something, but my leg was hurting, perhaps as a result of an injury that I had picked up on another walk, so I stayed in camp to rest my leg and hoped that it would be better for my next trek. I would have had a lie-in as I had a free day, but it was difficult when there was another overland truck that was packing up to leave at 5.30am and another overland truck packed up to leave at 6.30am. By that time, I was wide awake, so I got up and made some breakfast.

I went for a short walk to the local village. But outside the gates of the camp were a number of souvenir sellers, and you had to run the gauntlet of insistent sellers, hoping for their first sale of the day. They were friendly, but when you already have dozens of opportunities and don't want any of the items on offer, and they all sell a similar range of items, it is tiresome.

They all introduced themselves with names such as Norman, Ken, Tim, Morgan Freeman, or Mzu. The only things that I might be interested in were some black carved elephants to add to my daughter's collection, but those on offer were rather crudely carved. I was also intrigued by a traditional board game, which I know as owela from Namibia, but just about every country has different rules and different names. And none of the game boards on offer had the pieces; they were just the board with scoops for the stones or seeds used as counters. Apparently, I was expected to walk into the jungle and pick up the seeds or stones for myself.

There was a lot of noise from another overlanding truck, G Adventures, which was leaving at 5.30am. East Coast safaris are popular, and there are several companies offering tours. There are only a few campsites that are suitable, so it is not surprising that we might see other overlanding trucks at campsites and hostels.

We had a leisurely breakfast, left the mountains behind, and drove through some flat farmland, going northwards along the lake shore. We passed rice fields and some road construction crews who were building a new road, but whilst they were working on the improvement, the traffic was diverted onto a rough track that ran parallel to the construction site.

We stopped in the small town of Kalonwe to spend the last of our Malawi Kwacha before crossing the border into Tanzania, and this was another border where we had to show our yellow fever certificates, hand over our visa forms, passports, and USD 50, and wait whilst they processed our papers.

Conall had no dollars in cash and needed some hard currency for later. I wanted some Tanzanian shillings, so we made a deal. He got as many shillings out of an ATM at the border as he could, and I bought them with my dollars. The clocks had gone forward as well, so by the time we got to a suitable lunch site away from the border, it was well past three o'clock.

The ancient people of present-day Tanzania had been associated with the production of iron. The Pare people were the main producers of iron for tribes that occupied the mountain regions of northeastern Tanzania. The Haya people on the western shores of Lake Victoria had invented a type of blast furnace that allowed them to forge carbon steel at temperatures exceeding 1,820 °C more than

1,500 years ago, and these products were traded across the area. Travellers and merchants from the Persian Gulf and as far afield as India had discovered and traded on the East African coast since early in the first millennium AD.

European involvement in the area started with the German East Africa Company in 1884, which was formerly called the Society for German Colonisation, with the aim of trading in Africa. In 1885, the company leased the coastal strip opposite Zanzibar from Sultan Khalifa bin Said for 50 years. He was an Omani who had captured and colonised the island of Zanzibar and made it his capital in 1840, where it became the centre for the Arab slave trade.

The German East Africa Company's attempt to take over the administration of the area led to a general revolt along the coast of what is now Tanzania. The company could only hold Dar es Salaam and Bagamoyo with the help of the German navy. In 1889, it had to request the assistance of the German government to put down the rebellion. In 1891, after it became apparent that the company could not control its dominions, it passed much of its responsibilities to the German government, and this began the German colonisation and rule of the area that became to be known as German East Africa. The company initially continued to operate its many activities, including mines, plantations, railways, and banking, before it consented to relinquish them to the German colonial administration.

Caravans plied the interior, and there were people ready to extend European control into the interior. There were German caravans in the interior, such as those led by Tom von Prince and Wilhelm Langheld, but there was also competition from others, such as Emin Pasha from Turkey and Charles Stokes from Great Britain.

In 1890, London and Berlin concluded the Heligoland-Zanzibar Treaty, which returned Heligoland to Germany, made it important for the Imperial German Navy to have control over the exit to the North Sea of the newly built Kiel Canal, and gave Zanzibar to Great Britain, plus a resolution to a number of other boundary and sphere of influence issues. The treaty also handed the Caprivi Strip in Namibia to the then-German colony of Germany's Southwest Africa.

Between 1891 and 1894, the Hehe people, led by Chief Mkwawa, resisted German expansion. They were defeated because rival tribes supported the Germans. After years of guerrilla warfare, Mkwawa himself was cornered and committed suicide in 1898.

German colonial administrators relied heavily on native chiefs to keep order and collect taxes. By 1st January 1914, aside from local police, the military garrisons of Schutztruppen at Dar es Salaam, Moshi, Iringa, and Mahenge numbered 110 German officers (including 42 medical officers), 126 non-commissioned officers, and 2,472 Askari, a local African term for natives enlisted in European-controlled armies.

The Germans promoted commerce and economic growth. Over 40,000 hectares were put under sisal cultivation, which was the largest cash crop used in rope production. Two million coffee trees were planted, rubber trees were planted on 81,000 hectares, and there were large cotton plantations. In order to move all this produce, the Usambara Railway, covering 1,247 kilometres, was built from Tanga to Moshi with construction starting in 1888, linking Dar es Salaam, Morogoro, Tabora, and Kigoma.

Industrial gold mining in Tanzania in modern times dates back to gold discoveries near Lake Victoria in 1894. The Kironda Goldminen Gesellschaft established the first gold mine in the colony at the Sekenke Gold Mine, which began operation in 1909 after the finding of gold there in 1907. It was an underground mine, reaching up to 200 metres below the surface. The gold mine was the largest single producer of gold in what is now present-day Tanzania,

The mine closed in 1959, but during its time, it produced 140,000 ounces of gold plus, over 22,000 ounces of silver. Exploration rights in the area of the old mine now lie with Barrick Gold, and the industry has opened other mines in the area, but the Sekenke Mine was never reopened. During the First World War, gold from Sekenke was used to mint coins to pay German troops fighting against the allied forces.

The story of the German forces in East Africa is fascinating for its sheer tenacity. At the outbreak of the First World War in August 1914, the army was under the command of General Paul von Lettow-Vorbeck, who had served in Germany, Southwest Africa, and Kamerun, present-day Cameroon. His total forces consisted of 3,500 Europeans, mostly Germans, and 12,000 native Askaris. Their war strategy was to harry the British Imperial army of 40,000, which was at one time commanded by the former Second Boer War commander Jan Smuts.

One of Lettow-Vorbeck's greatest victories was at the Battle of Tanga in November 1914. This was the ocean terminus of the Usambara Railway, and reinforcements were brought in by train to counter the British amphibious landings. This battle is also called the Battle of the Bees, as a swarm of bees attacked the troops, both German and British, causing the attacking British troops to run away. The British suffered a severe defeat when the German forces defeated a British force more than eight times larger.

The British retreated but left a lot of their equipment behind, and Lettow-Vorbeck was able to re-equip three Askari companies with modern rifles, for which he now had 600,000 rounds of ammunition. He also had sixteen more machine guns, valuable field telephones, and enough clothing to last the Schutztruppe for a year. The British Official History of the War has called this one of the most notable failures in British military history. Casualties on the British side were 360 killed and 487 wounded, whilst the Schutztruppe side 16 Germans and 55 Askaris were killed and a total of 76 wounded.

The SMS Königsberg had been deployed to East Africa in April 1914 for a two-year deployment, but this was interrupted in August 1914 with the outbreak of the First World War. The ship initially attempted to raid British and French commercial traffic in the region, but only destroyed one merchant ship in the course of her career. Coal shortages hampered her ability to put it to sea and to attack shipping. On 20th September 1914, she surprised and sank the British cruiser HMS Pegasus in the Battle of Zanzibar.

She was eventually scuttled in the Rufiji delta in July 1915 after running low on coal and spare parts, and was subsequently blockaded and bombarded by the British navy. The surviving crew stripped out the remaining ship's guns and mounted them on gun carriages before joining the land forces, adding considerably to the Lettow-Vorbeck artillery's effectiveness.

Lettow-Vorbeck's guerrilla warfare tactics compelled Britain to commit significant resources to a minor colonial theatre throughout the war, which inflicted more than 10,000 casualties. Eventually, the weight of allied numbers, especially after forces coming from the Belgian Congo, had attacked from the west from present-day Rwanda and Burundi at the Battle of Tabora, 200 kilometres south of Lake Victoria, and dwindling supplies forced Lettow-Vorbeck to abandon the colony.

He withdrew south towards Portuguese Mozambique. The Portuguese army engaged the Germans whilst they were encamped at Ngomano on 25th November 1917. From here, the German troops moved into Northern Rhodesia, present-day Zambia. It was here that he agreed to a ceasefire three days after the end of the war in Europe after receiving news of the armistice that was signed in

Versailles that ended the war on the 11th hour of the 11th day of the 11th month in 1918.

Lettow-Vorbeck and his small army of European and locally recruited troops held out against much bigger forces for all four years of the Great War in Europe that had raged in France, and those allied troops and resources facing him were desperately needed in the European theatre. He was acclaimed after the war as one of Germany's heroes. His Schutztruppe was celebrated as the only colonial German force during World War I that was not defeated in open combat, although they often retreated when outnumbered. The Askari colonial troops who had fought in the East African campaign were later given pension payments by the Weimar Republic and West Germany.

Chapter 9
Ferry to Zanzibar

Education is the most powerful weapon that you can use to change the world.
Nelson Mandela

A man does not wander from where his maize is roasting.
Nigerian proverb

The road followed a ridge that rose high into some mountains, and we had broad scenic views from both sides of the truck. We were approaching three peaks that rose to between 2,100 metres and 2,600 metres. The soils were fertile, and at altitude, they got more rain and less of the shearing heat of the lowlands, so everything was a lush green colour. There were masses of banana palms and rows of cassava being grown on the ridges of the earth. There were also tea gardens galore, some were small, whilst others seemed to cover whole hillsides.

We turned off the main road to get to camp at Bongo Camping. It was a long drive up a rough track past several small farms, but people waved and smiled as we passed. This was a community enterprise run by the village in the former schoolhouse, and the villagers took it in turns to run the site, but when foreigners turn up, it is usually the teenagers who work, as they are more confident in speaking a foreign language. The grass was mown, smooth, and ideal for pitching a tent.

The facilities were basic but clean, but the toilet was a squat toilet, and there was only cold water in the showers. At lower altitudes, a cold shower is a pleasure and a relief from the heat, and the ambient temperature of the water is not such a shock to the system. But up here in the mountains, the water was cold, and the air temperature is cold, so a shower is more of a quick functional activity to get clean. The sun was shining, but when it was obscured by a cloud, the temperature would drop noticeably. It was unlikely to rain, but it was going to be a cold night.

In fact, it was a very cold night. The clouds blew over, and the stars twinkled until the full moon rose and drowned out the stars. The temperature plummeted, and there was heavy dew. I had a disturbing night as my Thermorest developed a leak and deflated during the night, leaving me lying on hard ground. The cockerels crowed all night, the dogs barked, and it was cold, Conall and James stayed up most of the night drinking, and their voices got louder as the evening got later until they went to bed at 3.30am. Conall was a night owl and would often sleep on the beach during the day but stay up until late into the early hours of the morning.

We drove up into some hills. The ground is hilly but very fertile and supported a range of crops. They grew potatoes, maize, tomatoes, beans, green beans, tea, and wheat. Some of the areas were forested with pine trees. For a while, a railway track ran parallel to the road, with mountains on one side and rolling plains on the other side. We crossed a river, and then there were roadworks. The road was being upgraded, but work was interrupting the smooth traffic flow. It would be a great improvement when it was completed, but we bumped along on temporary surfaces on one side of the construction site.

We passed through Mafinga and turned off the road to camp at Kizolanza Farm. It was a lovely, well fenced camp site, with hot water and a blazing fire, but the toilet facilities were just three long drop toilets. We had all got used to these, and often they didn't even cause a comment. But I always noticed. I was paranoid that something might drop out of my pockets, and I was not going to go rummaging around in a dark hole. My toilet routine took a different pattern with long drops, and I would empty my pockets or make sure that the zips on my fleece were closed so that there was no danger of anything dropping out.

Kizolanza Farm is a working cattle and sheep farm that also grows tobacco, vegetables, and flowers. It is a great destination, and they have chalets and a guest house. But all of that was somewhere else, and I only discovered the full range of facilities later. As we were camping, we followed the signs to the camp site and missed the main facilities. There was a bar and several huts around the campsite, but we were camping and were not even offered any upgrades.

We set off early to take the road via Iringa, Mikube, and finally Morogoro, through some fantastic scenery as we crossed the plateau and finally through Mikube National Park, which was established in 1964 and is the fourth largest in the country. It is home to giraffes, lions, elephants, zebras, impala, eland, kudu, black antelope, baboons, wildebeests, and buffaloes, but we would be very lucky to see any as we were just driving through on the main road, but we did see elephants and impala from the truck. We weren't able to take any photos as we didn't have a photo licence, and there were big fines imposed if you took a photo without a licence.

There are distinct eco systems here. It was a flat, rolling plain with some hard rock granite hills rising up out of the plain. We left the grasslands and headed down a dramatic, steep valley leading off the plateau into the jungle. There were several wrecks on the side of the road, and in one place, two crane trucks were picking up two smashed vehicles and various parts that had come off the main vehicle and placing the main wreck and parts onto low-loaders.

Heavy lorries were going down very slowly, and there were a lot of squeaking brake pads. It was a long and gradual descent, but all the professional lorry drivers were keeping their vehicles under control and not risking any speed. Impatient car drivers would overtake on blind bends and hope for the best. Gareth took it carefully, waited until he could see enough empty road, and then accelerated to overtake the slow lorries.

Hitting any animal in the park is against local bylaws, and errant drivers can be fined. There were signs to advise how much you would be fined if you hit any of the animals with the numbers in USD. The warthog was 150, impala 507, hyena 550, zebra 1,200, wildebeest 1,500 and elephant 15,000. Also, there were a lot of sections where there was a 30 kmph limit imposed, so we had to go slow, but we were not able to take photos and were not allowed to stop to see the wildlife.

It was slow going, so we were late reaching Morogoro and had no time to look around the city, the country's largest city and commercial centre, and 260 kilometres east of Dodoma, the country's capital city. Therefore, we went straight to our campsite on the outskirts of the city.

It was a new camp site, a long way from the centre, but it had plenty of tree cover for shade, although it was overcast and it rained during the night. The site was fenced, and the gate was guarded by armed security. We used one of the fire pits to avoid burning the grass or singeing the trees. We cooked shepherd's pie using soya instead of meat, so it was vegan and suitable for all. However, some soya products have too much salt, but this brand was less laced with salt, so it was better than some that we had used in the past. Some people mistake salt for flavour and will always add salt out of habit.

We were up in the dark for a 7am departure. We stopped at a servo for a pee and some coffee. I also bought a large packet of cashews and proceeded to eat the majority of the 500-gramme pack by the time that we reached Dar es Salaam.

The traffic was awful, but apparently it always is according to Kim and Gareth. We crossed the city and through an industrial area and passed some marshalling yards to cross a new bridge over the estuary that takes 20 kilometres off the previous journey. It took two hours to get across the city to our camp site on the beach just south of the port. We had left the cooking group of Mat, Sarah, and Jacci, plus Heather and David, near the ferry port to shop for the evening meal, and no doubt they would check out a bar before catching a taxi to the camp site.

We had a free afternoon, which was mainly spent at the bar, first getting some lunch, but it seemed no one really wanted to do anything else. The plates were cleared away, but nobody moved. Eventually, I left to have a shower and do some laundry. We had been warned that the local area is not safe as there have been a number of muggings, including some with threats of violence and knives, which sort of puts people off going anywhere unless you are in a group.

When the cook group Heather and David returned, in two tuk-tuks and boisterous from drink, I, Noodles, and Zac took one of the tuk-tuks to get back to the local shops to go to an ATM and the liquor store. It was David's birthday, so we were going to celebrate. Heather was baking a cake, and Laura was making bread and butter pudding, a rarity as we seldom did desserts other than perhaps a piece of fruit. Noodles got a bottle of champagne and some Campari; I bought a bottle of whisky and some wine.

By the time we got back, the cook group was well into cooking, and most of the others were at the bar. Heather had some balloons, so I blew them up whilst she cooked. Some people had not moved from the bar, so it seemed that it was going to be a busy and perhaps raucous night. The meal was great, and everyone continued celebrating David's birthday well into the night.

In the morning, we left the truck at the camp site and got a bus from the camp site to the ferry terminal for the five-minute crossing to the far side of the port. Then it was a walk of 1.3 kilometres from the commuter ferry to the ferry to reach Zanzibar. We queued in the strengthening glare of the sun to have our tickets and passport checked before we could enter the port area.

We sat in a holding area of long rows of chairs under a canvas canopy to keep the sun off until they were ready to receive passengers. It was a scramble to get aboard. We had allocated seats on the middle deck according to the tickets, but in reality, it was free seating as none of the seats had a number. We sat at the front to get a great view of the journey to come.

We followed the coast for an hour and then cut across the ocean towards Zanzibar. We saw several ships steaming along the coast, and it seemed to be a busy shipping channel. We came to Zanzibar's port with a large container port on one side.

We were met by our local minder, Daniel, who directed us to our transport to take us on a tour of a spice farm and ultimately to the north end of the island. Sarah, Mat, Chris, and Laura hired a car for a few days, picked it up at the ferry terminal, and followed Daniel. It was comical to see four adults in a small car, and it looked cramped, but Laura had volunteered to do the driving and probably had the most space. The first stop was lunch, and Daniel took us past David Livingstone's house to his own home for a traditional meal of ginger spiced beef, rice with potatoes, spinach cooked in coconut milk, and a vegetable curry with a piquant sauce.

Then we moved on to a local spice farm. Here they grow a whole range of spices, for which the islands are so well known. Few of the spices are indigenous to the area, but it has a warm climate with plenty of rain and fertile soils, so it is ideal for agriculture. There was a lack of labour to run the farms, but that was resolved by importing slaves.

We were told about how bananas grow and how they are looked after, and about cardamom plants, jackfruit, turmeric, cinnamon, vanilla, ginger, aloe vera, pineapples, cloves, and coconuts. And of course, loads of other plants such as yland ylang, black pepper, kapok, teak, cocoa, oil palm, and durian fruits. I had heard about these, but I had never tried one. The durian is distinctive for its large size, strong odour, and thorn-covered rind. The fruit can grow as large as 30 centimetres long and 15 centimetres in diameter, and it typically weighs one to three kilograms. Its shape ranges from oblong to round, the colour of its husk ranges from green to brown, and its flesh from pale yellow to red, depending on the species.

Then it was an hour's drive up the island to get to the northern point and our hotel accommodation. It was a marvellous location, right on the beach, and after what seemed like months of camping, we had a few nights in beds in chalets.

There were booze cruises on offer, trekking, snorkelling, fishing at sea, and of course, the option to sit and do nothing.

The first evening was the opportunity to go on a sunset booze cruise, but I decided that I didn't need to be on a boat to have a drink, so I stayed on land and had a few leisurely beers and chatted with other guests at the bar whilst watching the sun slowly dip below the horizon. The cruise was billed as 'free drinks' and 'as much as you can drink' with the cost of the drinks included in the ticket price. Conall and James took this as a challenge and got their money's worth. They reappeared a long time after dusk, and after the other cruise passengers had returned, they staggered along the beach and had to be helped to find their chalet.

It was another leisurely day doing nothing. Heather and David had taken off to go to another resort with Sarah, Mat, Laura, and Chris. Heather and David took a taxi, and the other four squeezed into their small hire car, but it was only a short journey, so the cramped conditions didn't matter. So, it was a smaller group than when we were in the truck. I hired a small sailing boat and went for a sail along the coast for an afternoon. On my return, I walked to the local shops, got a bottle of wine, and went back to the resort. I cooled it as best I could by running it under the cold tap.

After several days at the beach resort, we took the transfer from Nungwi Inn Resort to Stone Town to stay in the main town in Zanzibar and to be near the port for the return ferry to the mainland.

We were to stay at the Safari Lodge Hotel, which was just a short walk from the container port and the ferry terminal. We were met by our local minder, Daniel, again. The Stone Town streets are narrow, two people can pass, or a motorbike can squeeze past, but nothing larger can negotiate the streets. Our transfer dropped us off on the outskirts of the city, and Daniel showed us down the back streets to our hotel.

We had a few minutes to check in, and then six of us went for a city tour with Daniel, whilst the others had a short tour with Daniel's colleague to orient themselves and show them how to get to the Six Degrees restaurant for the group evening meal.

Daniel showed us the textile market and then the central market, built by the British starting in 1904 but not finished until 1907. There is a fish section, a meat section, a spice section, and a fruit and vegetable section, although there are so many traders that they have spread out to the outside walls of the original building.

We saw the original missionary's building and the extension on the other side of the road. Around the corner is the site of the former slave trading market. Zanzibar was a slave (as well as a gold, ivory, and spice) trading centre. There is an interesting slave museum. A couple of slave dungeons still exist. There is now a large Anglican cathedral built on the original site, and on the grounds is a monument to the thousands of slaves shipped from here.

The sultan, or at least his advisors, saw the islands as an ideal location for growing spices due to their warm weather and rainfall. There were extensive plantations, and the archipelago became known as the Spice Islands. Many of the slaves were set to work on the plantations. As many as 20% died in any one year, so there was always a need for more slaves.

The West African slave trade was largely concerned with shipping slaves to the Caribbean and the Americas. Many of the Zanzibar slaves rounded up on the east coast of the continent were used on local plantations or shipped to Arabia for domestic service.

We scouted out several good quality hotels, all former palaces or merchants' houses and now expensive hotels. We were shown where we would be having our evening group meal at the Six Degrees restaurant, and we would have to remember how to navigate through the streets to find it again. It was nice but a little expensive, so for our lunch, we found a more modestly priced vegetarian restaurant nearby.

Our stops after lunch included the fort built by the Portuguese but stormed by the Omani Arabs, who took over control of the islands. Part of today is an amphitheatre where music festivals are held, and another part has been left as it was and is now a tourist souvenir market. Some of the buildings with functional roofs today house the tourism information ministry.

Next door is the Omani Palace, a large building in need of some renovation and repair, especially after a corner of the roof was ripped off in a recent storm. A few timbers had been erected as scaffolding, and a piece of tarpaulin had been stretched across some of the worst affected areas. There are plans and money is available, partly donated from Oman, but restoration work has not yet started.

By the end of the tour, there was only an hour before we were due back at the restaurant for the happy hour drinks before our evening meal. There is always a temptation to drink too much, as cocktails seem to be so colourful, moreish, and deceptive in that the fruit juices disguise the alcohol content. You can easily have several before alcohol starts reaching the brain, speech becomes impaired, and hand-to-eye coordination plummets.

I was saved by the fact that I was getting hungry, so I took myself off to find something to eat at another restaurant. I like a glass of wine with my meal, but I regret leaving Six Degrees. I found several menus with attractive fish options, but being a 98% Muslim island, they were all dry. I ended up eating at the night market. I had a selection of prawns, lobster and kingfish for a lot less than I was prepared to pay in a hotel restaurant.

I was back at the hotel early and had an early night. Breakfast was at 7.30am and I wandered down a few back streets until our departure time to leave the hotel at 11am and walk to the nearby ferry port. We dutifully filled in our emigration cards, showed our yellow fever cards, and had our passports checked. Some of us were also asked to complete a tourism questionnaire about our stay, including questions on how much we had spent and what and where.

I didn't make a note of any of these details, as I wasn't aware that I might be asked. Therefore, it was a bit of fiction, but I did my best. For instance, when I booked and paid for a tour, how can I split the cost between the transport, the guide, the food on offer, and the entrance fee? And I bet there were a few drinks, street food, or souvenir costs that I forgot.

The islands of Zanzibar and mainland Tanzania are the same country, but they were administered separately in colonial times. The former mainland Tanganyika became independent in 1961, and the Zanzibar Archipelago became independent in 1963. In 1964, the two countries merged, and the new country was renamed Tanzania. However, we still had to show our passports and receive a stamp.

It was one of the roughest crossings I have ever experienced. It was a fast twin hulled boat, but the wind was strong, and there were giant rollers coming from the southeast all the way from Antarctica hitting our port bow, making us pitch and yore violently.

There were children and adults crying, people being sick, people moaning and lying on the floor, the sounds of people retching and gagging, and sick bags being handed out by the crew like confetti. It was too windy and wet to stand on deck, so everyone was inside. We were all glad to get back on land and away from the boat. Some still hadn't recovered after reaching land. Oddly, none of our group was affected except for Kenny, and it was an odd sense of amusement that, whilst we were all okay, it had affected all the local Africans so badly.

Gareth was there near the dockside with Nala to pick us up, but we had to walk a kilometre to where he was parked at the railway station, as that was the closest that he could find nearby the ferry to park and wait for us. He drove north out of town, 60 kilometres up the coast, to reach our camp site in Bagamoyo.

Today, the ferries go from Dar es Salaam to the island of Zanzibar, but at the time of the slave trade, slave caravans would terminate at Bagamoyo. The town was founded in the 18th century and later became the capital of German East Africa from 1886 to 1891, when the capital was moved to Dar es Salaam, although there had been a settlement here for centuries for fishermen and farmers trading fish, salt, gum, and later ivory and slaves. Caravans from the interior would make their way here as it developed into a major commercial port in the 19th century. In fact, the name means "take the load off and rest".

The slaves brought by the caravans would be shipped to Zanzibar for sale in its slave market. Bagamoyo's architecture for both its fort and some of the secular buildings is very similar to Stone Town in Zanzibar, which is not surprising because they were developed and built in the same decades.

The city was also the starting place for many caravans heading into the interiors and it was the starting place for several famous explorers such as Richard Burton, John Speke, Henry Stanley, and James Grant. Contrary to popular belief, David Livingstone never visited the place during his lifetime; he was laid out in the Old Church's tower (nowadays named Livingston Tower) before being shipped to Zanzibar. From there, his body was shipped to London, and he was buried in Westminster Abbey in 1874, a year after he died.

Chapter 10
Ngorongoro Crater and Serengeti

After climbing a great hill, one only finds that there are many more hills to climb.
Nelson Mandela

A goat is never pronounced innocent if the judge is a leopard.
A Kru proverb from Liberia

We got up in the dark for a long drive day to go from Bagamoyo to the Marangu Hotel, which is in the foothills of Kilimanjaro. We set off and drove all day. We were stopped at 11am by the police for allegedly speeding. It is a common tactic to stop lorries and cars and charge a fine. Gareth is extremely careful and always follows the speed limit. It is also an old and heavy truck and can't go fast. I was reminded of the Skoda joke, "What do you call a Skoda going at 80 kmph? A miracle". He would also lose his job and his licence, so he is always careful.

The police alleged that he was speeding, and he was confident that he wasn't. There was an impasse. We got off the truck and looked around the immediate area, as we knew that it would take time. The police often rely on people just paying to get on with their journey, but we had a rule that we would not pay bribes or excessive amounts over the odds. Besides, every penny has to be accounted for, and it would come out of the budget. We knew the score, so we had at least an hour before the police lost interest. I walked up the road to a local market. There were fruit and vegetables, soft drinks, and clothes for sale. I was feeling hungry, so I bought two large avocados for the equivalent of less than 20 pence. They are expensive at home, but they are cheap and abundant here.

When I got back to the truck, nothing had happened, so Gareth pulled off the road and parked the truck in some shade where the police cars were parked. It was lunchtime, so we set up the kitchen for lunch next to a police 4x4. It was being made clear that we would not pay a bride (…such a harsh word, but they called it a 'fine' but would not give a receipt), and it was equally obvious that we were in no hurry to get on with our journey. We also outnumbered the police and milled around in the shade of the tree that they were parked under. They were friendly and chatted, but having started the speeding 'fine' process, they couldn't back down easily.

They couldn't do their job when they were inundated with foreigners milling about and getting in their way. We were also a source of fascination for some of the locals, and despite the police, several came over to look at what was going on, and the police were having trouble stopping other vehicles for 'fines' with so many people milling about and witnesses. We were also causing traffic to slow down anyway to see what was happening, and the police lost interest in us. Eventually they decided to give Gareth a verbal warning and wanted us out of their way. We finished our lunch, cleared up, and set off again, with no bribes, oops, my mistake, without any 'fine' being paid.

With such an early lunch, it was a long afternoon. We passed through plantations of sisal. It used to be grown in huge quantities until sisal was replaced with much cheaper plastic ropes, the price of sisal fell, and farmers went out of business. There is still a market for it, but the quantity grown is nothing like it used to be. Production peaked in 1964 at over 230,000 tons but average annual production over the last ten years has been about 25,000.

The rolling plains changed to mountains as we got nearer Kilimanjaro. There were peaks in the distance, and soon we were driving under the lee of a range of mountains. Then the road rose into the mountains, the temperature dropped, and it felt damp as we climbed. It looked like rain.

We drove into the Marangu Hotel. It has several chalets set in beautifully manicured gardens and a large green lawn. The rooms are spacious, quiet, and cool, but despite the luxury, we would be camping around the back of the hotel, unless, of course, you paid for an upgrade. James and Mike nearly always upgraded. I did occasionally, and a few of the others I don't remember ever upgrading to, such as Kenny and Kristin.

When there was an option to upgrade, there was always some space available, but it is often more of a budget issue, and after several nights in beds on Zanzibar, it was hard work to set up a tent and sleep on the ground, and being at altitude, it would be a cold night. With the extra time spent at the police roadblock, it was getting dark as we set up the kitchen and the tents. But then we left the cook group preparing the meal, and the rest of the group retired to the comfort of the hotel bar to wait for our supper of stuffed peppers to be ready.

This was a chance to chill and relax after experiencing the culture of Zanzibar. I walked into town, but there wasn't much there. It had one bank and an ATM; there were several shops and not much else. A local welcomed me to his country and said that my friends were having coffee over the road. I wondered how he knew that they were my friends, but white faces are unusual, and they know that there are groups of travellers. By the time that I got to the café, they had moved on, but without asking, the owner said that my friends had gone down the road. I gave up the chase and just looked around the market and then walked the two kilometres back down the road to the hotel.

I had lunch in the bar and tried some of the local wine. Jacci said she liked it, but it wasn't to my palate. That afternoon, another overlanding truck arrived with a group of just twelve. It is always interesting to meet other overlanders and compare stories, especially if they are doing a similar tour. We kicked a ball around on the lawn and then had a match of our truck verses their truck. I can't remember who won, or even who was ahead before it degenerated into a farce, and we retired to the bar.

Most of us had had breakfast and packed up. All except Noah, who missed breakfast and was the last to pack up. We said goodbye to the other truck and waved as they drove out of the hotel grounds. We were ready to go as well, but Noah was still packing away his tent, so we gave him a hand and set out ourselves, a little later than had been planned.

As we headed north, we stopped on the side of the road to get a look at Mount Kilimanjaro. It was a cloudy day, but we could just make out the grey smudge at the base of the cloud where the lower slopes were. The cloud cover wasn't continuous, and sometimes we caught glimpses of the peak, but we never saw the whole thing.

We stopped in Arusha for shopping and lunch. Then we got back on the road to get to Meserani Snake Park, where we planned to meet up with another sister truck. They had arrived the day before and had already set up their tents, but they were away from the camp when we arrived. Gareth parked up adjacent to the other truck, and we unpacked and carried everything that we might need from the truck to the barbecue pit situated conveniently next to the bar.

We had some spare time before lighting the fire, so we got the bird book out and tried to identify just some of the many colourful birds on site. The camp site was called Meserani Snake Park. There is a campground, and some upgrades are available but the big thing here is that they have several types of snakes and support the local snake venom project. Profits from the bar go to support the project, so we were drinking for charity.

You can wander through the snake enclosures and view the snakes in their enclosures and cages. There are pythons, cobras, and black and green mambas, plus a host of other snakes too numerous to mention. There are also some snakes in open pits with high concrete sides. Each cage and enclosure had its snakes carefully named in English and Latin on signs, plus some detail about their typical habits and range.

I was up early and cleared away the mess from the party before. As I got up, Conall was just going to bed. He had been awake all night. He talks loudly and doesn't seem able to talk in a quiet voice, so it was annoying if he had kept you awake as well. He stayed up with several others, but they slowly drifted away until it was just Conall and Phil from New Zealand from the other truck, which was originally called Woxy (after its number plate that starts WOX) but recently rechristened, but Woxy was such a good name that this is the one that stuck.

I went to look at the snakes again, but nothing much had changed, and I am sure that some of them hadn't moved from the first time that I had seen them. Then I walked out of the camp site to the local village, which was just a few shops, and a service station, and a police roadblock. There was an art gallery opposite the camp site where there was tanzanite jewellery for sale.

Tanzanite is a blue and violet variety of the mineral zoisite, caused by small amounts of vanadium, and is only found in Tanzania, in a very small mining area (approximately seven kilometres long and two kilometres wide) near the Merelani Hills. The scientific name of "blue violet zoisite" was not thought to be consumer friendly enough by Tiffany & Co.'s marketing department, which introduced it to the market in 1968, so they renamed it 'tanzanite' after Tanzania, the country in which it was discovered. The art gallery also had a lot of African art and crafts. I really wanted a large wooden animal, something large enough to sit on, but at prices between USD 2,500 and USD 11,000, they are not an impulse buy. And it would cost a lot to ship it home, a service that the shop thoughtfully provides in house.

Noah was going about his stomach. He is such a negative person and rarely seems to have anything positive to say. He was talking about his diarrhoea and that he had gone thirty times yesterday and thirty times the day before and was already into double figures today. Someone said sotto voce so that he didn't hear that he always talked so much bullshit that if he kept his mouth shut, he could easily get it down to single figures.

From here, you can choose to go into the Ngorongoro Crater and Serengeti National Park for a day where vast herds of wildebeest roam the plains. It was expensive, but it was a once in a lifetime experience, and it was not within everyone's budget, so some stayed behind in Snake Camp. For those who wish to experience a Maasai village, there is a trip on offer to visit a local village and learn about their culture and way of life. It was only a moderate cost, but I was unhappy to poke around someone's house or hut and look at all their belongings, however cheap the cost of the tour might be, so that was another tour opportunity that I declined.

When the Serengeti area was created, many of the Maasai were relocated to Ngorongoro, but this just meant that there were more people and livestock competing with the wildlife. Further restrictions have been introduced to protect wildlife and limit pastoral activity. The result is that there are some great safaris to be had, but the locals still need to live. The Ngorongoro area is the only national park in Tanzania where human activity and settlements are allowed alongside wildlife.

We were picked up at lunchtime and driven for the four-hour journey to our eco lodge just outside of the gates of the Ngorongoro Conservation Area and its top attraction, the Ngorongoro Crater, a large volcanic caldera. The name of the crater has an onomatopoeic origin, as it was named by the Maasai pastoralists after the sound produced by the cowbell (Ngoro Ngoro). The idea was that we would camp near the gates, and then in the morning it would be just a fifteen-minute drive to the gates and the start of our game drive through the Ngorongoro Conservation Area. Game drives are best in the morning or evening when the animals are active, as they tend to rest in the heat of midday.

We had paid a lot for our safaris through the Ngorongoro and later, the Serengeti, and we were deeply disappointed with our hotel. The main building was a characterless concrete square with broken tiles on the floor, which were unsightly and a trip hazard. It had dual pricing in the bar. You could pay in US dollars, and I tried offering my smallest bill, a twenty, but they didn't have sufficient change, and I don't travel with a wad of small notes. If you paid in local currency, the price was 25% more, rounded up significantly to the next convenient number, and again, they didn't have change, but luckily, I had some small local notes, so I bought a drink and decided not to buy any more.

There was a large pool, but it cost an extra five dollars. I wasn't tempted, not due to the price, but I couldn't see the bottom, so I wasn't convinced that it was a healthy option. The staff were all friendly and polite, but it didn't cancel out the fabric of the building or the pricing of the services that they provide.

There was worse to come as we were camping on the grounds, and the camp site was at the bottom of a slope in the shade where there was no breeze and lots of biting insects lurked. There was the usual noise from the town plus four dogs who spent all night chasing each other around the site and growling, barking at each other, and making other imperceptible threats. Add in the noise from the local disco with its African beat and deep bass, and it is not a place that I would ever recommend. I would give it a zero out of five on the TripAdvisor review. Worst camp site ever.

We entered the Ngorongoro Conservation Area, and the road wound its way up the outside of the crater rim through thick rain forest. It was early in the morning, and there was a low cloud. There was so much cloud that when we reached the lookout point, there was no point in stopping as there was nothing to see. We came to a dip in the road, and in front of us was a depression that had a lake at the bottom. We were on the rim of the caldera, and this area is usually grass, but there had been so much rain just recently that there was a temporary lake in the dip.

Then we crossed the rim and descended into the caldera. The floor of the caldera is at an elevation of 1,800 metres, and the steep inner sides tower up to 610 metres above the floor of the crater. It was a massive volcano, and it is estimated to have been up to 5,800 metres high until its last eruption, which emptied the magma chamber and caused the cone to collapse in upon itself. The flat floor of the caldera is up to 22 kilometres wide and covers over 260 square kilometres.

No Europeans are known to have set foot in the Ngorongoro Crater until 1892, when it was visited by Oscar Baumann, an Austrian explorer and cartographer. On this expedition, he was also the first European to enter Rwanda, and to visit Lakes Eyasi and Manyara. He has a street named after him in Vienna, Baumannstraße.

The crater is known for its wildlife, and there are black rhinoceros, Cape buffalo, hippopotamus, Grant's and Thomson's gazelles, blue wildebeest, Grant's zebras, and eland. There are no crocodiles, as the sides are too steep for them to negotiate their way into the crater. There are also no giraffes, one guidebook says that it is because of the steep sides, but it is more likely to be due to the lack of plants that the giraffes like to graze.

Low clouds hugged the rim, but the weather cleared as we descended into the crater. On our safari, the first large animals that we saw were some wildebeest and an eland. There were a pair of crested cranes, the national bird of Uganda, Thomson's gazelle, and a spotted hyena. We saw a hippopotamus out of the water and hurried over to get a photo, but by the time we got there, it had headed back to the water and was just submerging as I got my camera out and adjusted the lens to focus.

We passed a single male lion making its way through the long grass towards the road. It had a lot of scars on its back and flanks, and it must have had several fights with other males for supremacy. When he was younger, he probably was an alpha male, but now that he was getting old, his treasured position had been usurped. He was also thin, and his ribs showed. Lions usually hunt for pride, with the females doing most of the work, so life for a single male is tough.

There were plenty of other safari vehicles in the park, and whenever you see one stopped at the side of the track, there is probably something to see. When there are several vehicles parked nose to tail, there is something big to see. We joined a throng of safari vehicles to view some lions. This was a group of females and youngsters who had been stalking some game, but they had been seen, and the game had run off. The pride was crossing the road in between the stationary vehicles. They took no notice of us as they threaded their way in between the vehicles. We had some incredible views of them as they made their way past us and up the slope to rest on some rocky outcrops overlooking the road.

No sooner had we turned around and left that pride than we came across another large gathering of safari vehicles. This was another pride with males and females, and they had a kill. It was Cape buffalo, and as we approached the collection of vehicles, we saw a female pulling at the carcass. It was only when we got level with the kill that we had a surprise. There are very few trees in the crater, so there is little shade. So after the kill, and stuffing of their faces, the pride had walked over to the vehicle and laid down in the shade of several of the trucks. It was an amusing sight to see so many predators just lying next to the trucks, but it also meant that some vehicles couldn't move as they were trapped by the lions.

We moved off but soon stopped again. There was another male lion lying in a small hollow beside the road. We were standing in the back of the truck so we could look down, but if you were sitting in the front or in one of the smaller vehicles, the lion would be totally obscured by the tall grass.

Everywhere there were herds of hundreds of zebras, and walking across the road just ahead of us was a herd of five juvenile male elephants. Half the zebras leave the crater during the rainy season, as do a fifth of the wildebeest. In contrast, the numbers of buffalo and eland increase during the rainy season.

We stopped at one of the few places where you are allowed to get out of your vehicle. It was a picnic stop with toilets next to a small lake. There were some hippopotamus in the water on the far side of the lake, and some pelicans were swimming past the shore where we were standing.

Then we moved out of the crater, up the steep inner face of the cliffs, and drove on to the Serengeti. Here there were more trees and shrubs, and as we drove along the road, we passed several giraffes munching on the leaves at the tops of the trees.

The road to the Ngorongoro Crater was tarmac until it entered the park, and then it was just a rough track. The road between the two areas was also just a rough gravel track, and the vehicles threw up great clouds of dust as they shot along. Great clouds of dust were blown away by the light breeze, but if you drove too close to the vehicle in front, you would be covered in dust. Drivers would wait at some distance from the truck to avoid the dust cloud until there was a clear stretch of road, then accelerate to catch up with the truck, pass it, and once again have a clear view of the road in front.

We passed the gate and the start of Serengeti National Park. It was just an arch and a sign hanging from the centre of the arch. A Thomson gazelle walked across the road ahead, and then three cheetahs, two juveniles and a female, walked across the road in the same direction. They were stalking the gazelles.

The gazelle had noticed that it was being stalked and put in a little sprint, and the cheetahs stopped and laid down. The gazelle then slowed to a walk a little further but then changed direction. The cheetahs got up and walked through the long grass, gaining on the gazelle unnoticed. The gazelle started sprinting, followed by the three cheetahs.

One of the cheetahs accelerated and gained on the gazelle, and then the distance between them stayed the same, and the cheetah dropped back to be replaced by the other juvenile, who picked up speed and closed the gap with the gazelle. The same thing happened again with the gap closing but then staying the same as the gazelle matched the cheetah's speed.

The mother was then put in a sprint, and both juveniles slowed down. The gazelle was tiring, but the mother put in a determined sprint, much longer than the juveniles had run. The gap closed and closed, and then there was a puff of dust as the cheetah jumped onto the back of the prey and brought it to the ground.

The two juveniles walked up, and all three sat down to tear at the carcass. We saw a kill, and it all took less than a couple of minutes. We had a grandstand view, and it was so close to us that we didn't even need binoculars. It all happened so fast that none of us got a photo or any video of the kill. We waited and watched for a while, but with the cheetahs lying down in the long grass, there was not much to see.

Occasionally, one of the cheetahs would sit up, and that was the only way that other vehicles might know that there were cheetahs there and a kill just off the road. I felt sorry for the gazelle, but then this is nature, and we were all thrilled to have seen the chase.

Further along, was another large herd of zebras. There were several pairs of animals standing shoulder to shoulder and resting their chins on the backs of the other zebra. This is a common sight, and they are literally watching each other's backs. Each can relax knowing that the other zebra is looking out for predators behind him.

We passed Lion Rock, a steep sided outcrop of rock sticking out of the flat grasslands. It is a favourite haunt of lions, and they can see a long way across the savannah. It is also a favoured position, especially after a kill. They stuff themselves and then lie down to sleep it off. They can sleep quite deeply, and if they were asleep in the grass and were discovered by elephants, the elephants would attack and crush the lions, so the lions prefer to sleep on rocks or in trees to avoid encounters with elephants.

We came across a scattering of safari trucks amongst several acacia trees. As we approached, we saw a cheetah sitting by a waterhole. Then suddenly, it got up and ran away. Then we saw that there was a leopard who had run towards the cheetah and had scared it off. So, we had a leopard chasing a cheetah, and the cheetah would always escape as it was faster, but it was also my first sighting of a leopard, which is one of the most difficult animals of the Big Five to see as it is elusive and often hunts at night, so it is difficult to get a sighting. I ticked off the last of the Big Five.

We waited to see whether we would get another view, but the leopard was adept at using cover, and it slunk down into the long, tall grass, and we couldn't see it. It was another ten minutes before we saw it again, but our patience paid off as we saw it climb a nearby tree. I hadn't seen it earlier, but there was a carcass hanging from the tree. It was a young buffalo that the leopard had killed. He had eaten what he wanted and then stashed away what was left in the tree. This may be what the cheetah was after, but the leopard was protecting its kill, and it would have chased and killed the cheetah if it wasn't so full of meat. We watched for a while, but there was unlikely to be any more activity as the leopard climbed into the tree and settled down to go to sleep after a large meal.

We had a great day driving through Ngorongoro and Serengeti and seeing some of the huge herds that migrate across the flat bottom of the caldera, but it was time to leave. We drove up the inner face of the crater and stopped at the viewpoint that we had passed in the morning. This time, there was a great view across the huge crater in the late afternoon sun. We drove through the jungle on the outside of the crater that had been shrouded in mist that morning. We stopped at the entrance to the park to stretch our legs and use the facilities before driving all the way back to Snake Camp.

We parked the truck and set up the kitchen, and most of the group went to the bar. Meanwhile, I went for a shower, but the water temperature was intermittent, oscillating from tepid to too hot and then suddenly plummeting to ambient cold water, so it was not a nice experience standing under the water in the shower.

We left Snake Camp and drove up to the border between Tanzania and Kenya. We got so used to slow border crossings that we knew what to expect and just had to use lots of patience, an attribute that I don't have in abundance when it seems so effortless to improve efficiency. But it was also an opportunity to buy some street food and change money, either hard currency or to exchange the last few notes of the country that you were just leaving. I always try to budget so that I do not have a lot of local currency left and nothing to spend it on, but it is inevitable that you have some local currency left. I, for one, never want to be in a position of not having any currency and wanting to buy something, even if it is just a drink or a meal. I tend to be over budget, so I am always left with some local currency to change.

Chapter 11
Tea and Flowers

If wealth was the inevitable result of hard work, then every African woman would be a millionaire.
George Monibot

He who is carried on another's back does not appreciate how far it is to the next city.
African proverb

We drove through rolling farmland away from the border and into the outskirts of Nairobi. We negotiated wide roads, flyovers, one-way systems, and past multi-storey buildings until we came to a well laid out green residential area with quiet, wide roads and large houses with large gardens hidden behind high, neatly trimmed hedges. I had soon lost my sense of direction, but Gareth drove confidently down identical roads to reach our destination at Karen Camping in Nairobi, the capital of Kenya. It was a nice area, but we were told not to go anywhere without a guard or a taxi.

Kenya's capital and largest city is Nairobi, whilst its oldest city and the original capital is the coastal city of Mombasa. Kisumu City is the third largest city and a critical inland port on Lake Victoria. Kenya's geographical and topographical diversity yields a variety of climates, including a warm and humid coastline, temperate savannah grasslands in the interior, temperate forested hilly areas in the west, arid and semi-arid areas near the Somali border, and an Equatorial climate around Lake Victoria, the world's largest tropical freshwater lake and the second-largest freshwater lake after Lake Superior. Kenya has an abundance of varied flora and fauna, many of which are protected by wildlife reserves and national parks.

European exploration of the interior began in the 19th century, with the British Empire establishing a protectorate in 1895. Kenya gained independence in December 1963. Kenya's economy is the largest in eastern Africa, with Nairobi serving as a major regional commercial hub. In 1899, it was just a swamp until a rail depot and marshalling yards were built here as part of the railway that ran from Mombasa on the coast to Kampala in Uganda. Sir George Whitehouse, a brilliant engineer who also constructed railways in Mexico, Peru, Argentina, South Africa, and India, chose the site as it had a favourable climate, being at altitude and situated just before the steep ascent up the Limuru escarpment. The settlement grew so fast that it replaced Mombasa as the capital in 1907.

During the early part of the 20th century, the interior central highlands were settled by British and other European farmers, who became wealthy growing coffee and tea. By the 1930s, approximately 30,000 white settlers lived in the area and gained a political voice because of their contribution to the market economy.

Throughout the Second World War, Kenya was an important source of manpower and agriculture for the allies and for the United Kingdom in particular. Kenya itself was the site of fighting between allied forces and Italian troops in 1940-41 when Italian forces invaded from Italian East Africa, made up of the present-day countries of Somalia, Ethiopia, and Eritrea, and bombed Wajir and Malindi before the attacking forces were repulsed and defeated.

From 1952 to 1959, Kenya was in a state of emergency arising from the Mau rebellion against British rule. One of several factors was the expansion of Nairobi, which angered both the Maasai and Kikuyu tribes as it was swallowing their agricultural land and making it an urban fringe. Mau, also known as the Kenya Land and Freedom Army, were primarily members of the Kikuyu tribe.

The capture of their leader, Dedan Kimathi, on 21st October 1956, in Nyeri signified the ultimate defeat of the Mau Mau and essentially ended the military offensive. Kenya became an independent country under the Kenya Independence Act 1963. Exactly 12 months later, on 12th December 1964, Kenya became a republic.

Agriculture is the largest sector, with tea and coffee being traditional cash crops, while fresh flowers are a fast-growing export, and with other agricultural produce, it makes up more than 40% of total exports. The service industry is also a major economic driver, in particular, tourism.

We were warned by the manager of the campgrounds that Nairobi was not safe and to go everywhere by car in at least two pairs, if not more. It rather puts you off going anywhere, even when the locals say it is dangerous. The cook group of Noodles, Chris, and I ordered a taxi to take us to the local shopping mall, and Noah came along for the ride to do some personal shopping.

There was security at the entrance to the shopping mall, and the taxi had a cursory search. The taxi parked in the shopping mall car park. We had booked the taxi to take us to the shops, wait until we had finished, and then take us back. We agreed that it would be an hour, which was more than necessary but gave everyone sufficient time, and the taxis were so cheap that it didn't cost much more for the taxi driver to sit and wait.

We then walked through another security control with a metal detector and received a more thorough search. Kenya has seen more than its fair share of terrorism-related incidents and has been the scene of various attacks. In 1980, the Jewish owned Norfolk hotel was attacked by the Palestine Liberation Organisation. In 1998, the US embassy in Nairobi was bombed by al Qaeda, as was the Israeli owned Paradise hotel in 2002. In 2013, the militant group Al-Shabaab killed 67 people at Nairobi's Westgate Shopping Mall, and there have been numerous other lesser attacks in addition to street crime, so there is armed security and checks everywhere.

We did all our cooking group shopping and noodles, and I carried everything back to the taxi and waited. Chris and Noah had gone to do some personal shopping. Chris soon rejoined us, and we waited for Noah. The agreed time came and went, and there was no sign of Noah. We checked the food hall in case he had stopped for a McDonald's. He was American and lived off fast food. We knew he wanted a phone shop, so we checked all those as well, but still no Noah. We tried using his phone, but it was turned off. Eventually, we couldn't wait any longer, so we went back without him. He turned up at the camp a few hours later, but no apology, no text, and he was not even returning to the taxi to tell us that he needed some more time shopping.

The next day was a public holiday for Ramadan, so some things would be shut but there was no consistency in what was open or not. Some of us got a taxi to visit the David Sheldrick Wildlife Trust and their elephant orphanage, just a few kilometres away at the western end of Nairobi National Park. Despite seeing elephants in the wild, it is still a great experience to see nursery animals come out for their daily mud baths and comical plays and to see the amazing work the centre does and has done with rescued and injured elephants and rhinoceros over the last 40 years.

Nearby is the Langata Giraffe Centre, where you can learn more about these gentle and majestic creatures with the opportunity to get up close to feed them from a raised platform. These are the endangered Rothchild giraffes that are only found on the grasslands of East Africa. There were also warthogs that shared the giraffe's enclosures. They aren't particularly attractive; in fact, some people say they are ugly, but you never forget your first encounter with a warthog.

We were lucky that these two tourist destinations were open, and we were confined over the phone that they were open, but some other places didn't answer the phone, so we guessed that they were shut. Some of the shops in the mall were shut. Driving down the streets, some market stalls were open, but there were many empty stalls, and there were fewer people on the streets, but at least there was less traffic that day.

When we left Nairobi, we said goodbye to Conall, who was continuing his journey by flying to Germany. He was still looking for work and had an open mind on what he was to do next, but his plan was to visit friends in Germany and see whether there were any job opportunities. But the group was the same size as Hazel, who had joined us in Nairobi. She was a teacher from Ireland who would be coming with us to Cairo. We headed northwest and reached the Eastern Great Rift Valley. The road dipped and crossed the face of the cliff down to the floor of the rift valley. Some inactive volcanoes were just visible through the morning mist that the sun had yet to burn off.

We stopped to shop in Naivasha and were met by our local fixer, Henry, and his sister Mary, who led us to the market, which was down several streets, and we would have never found it by ourselves. The markets were our preferred shopping option as they are cheaper than the supermarkets, but we couldn't always find everything that we wanted, so we bought all the vegetables first in the market and then went to the supermarket for meat, eggs, bread, and beans. There were plenty of beans in the market, but they were all dried and would have to be soaked overnight, and we wanted to use them the same day, so we had to find tinned beans.

We drove on to our campsite at Fishermen's Camp on the shores of Lake Naivasha within Lake Naivasha National Park. The camp site is on the shore of the lake, but there is a fence along the water's edge. There would be no swimming in the lake as there are hippopotamus here, and the fence is to keep the hippos out of the lush grass of the campground. We set up camp opposite a large shelter, which housed a barbecue pit, work surfaces, tables, and chairs.

There were activity options explained to us by Henry. There was bike hire to go for a cycle, with or without a guide, a chance to visit Hell's Gate National Park and a walk in a gorge, or a visit to Longonot National Park to walk up an inactive volcano and see the crater, known as the Crater Lake Game Sanctuary.

My first trip away from the camp was to visit Elsamere, Joy Adamson's home of Born Free fame, and her husband, George Adamson, who was the Senior Wildlife Warden of the Northern Frontier District. It is in a lovely setting overlooking Lake Naivasha. There is a small museum and an arboretum, and the house is surrounded by botanical gardens. It is now a hotel, but non-resident guests are welcome, and the hotel staff are happy to show guests a short film about Joy Adamson and her work with Elsa, the first of several projects with a lion and later with other big cats. The hotel serves afternoon tea on the lawn, and all profits help fund the charitable work of the Elsa Conservation Trust. The aim is to continue Joy Adamson's lifelong commitment to wildlife conservation, operating a wildlife retreat and an education centre at Adamson's former home, and essential work around the world. I had afternoon tea sitting on the lawn, watching the birds that flew around the garden.

It had promised to rain all afternoon. The forecast was for rain from 4pm with 100% certainty. Back in camp, we cooked under the awning, but the rain only hit us at 7pm, and it was the heavy monsoon type of rain. It was wet and cold, so some of us played Monopoly on the truck. The others had gone to the bar, which was more than 500 metres away, and there was no cover between the tents and the bar. Once it had started raining heavily, they were marooned there as they waited for the rain to ease off or stop.

The name Lake Naivasha derives from the local Maasai name Nai'posha, meaning "rough water" because of the sudden storms that can arise on this lake, which is just one of several in the Great Rift Valley. Its surface area covers 139 square kilometres, and its surface elevation is 1,884 metres with a maximum depth of 30 metres. It is fed by a number of streams and two large rivers. It has no outlet, but it is a freshwater lake, so it is assumed to have an underground exit. The level of the lake has varied over time and has shrunk to just a puddle several times in recent history.

There are over 400 bird species, but the fish species have been highly variable over time, influenced by changes in climate, fishing, and the introduction of invasive species. Common carp were accidentally introduced in 2001, and in just a decade, carp accounted for over 90% of the fish caught in the lake.

Just to the south of Lake Naivasha is Hell's Gate National Park, named after a narrow break in the cliffs called Njorowa Gorge, which used to form Lake Naivasha's outlet, but after tectonic activity, it is now high above the lake and forms the entrance to Hell's Gate National Park. There is also geothermal activity here, and in 1981, the first geothermal plant and the first of its kind in Africa was commissioned, and by 2000, there were three plants with a total of 45 MW of electricity being generated in the area. The area is home to lions, leopards, and cheetahs, but I didn't see any. For film buffs, the 2003 film Lara Croft's Tomb Raider: The Cradle of Life was shot on location in the park.

Whenever we stop somewhere for a few days, it is an opportunity to do a few essential jobs. Mine was to do some washing, and I was glad I didn't do it on the first day, otherwise; it would have been rained on, and with strong winds, it may have been blown off the washing line and land, in the mud and would need washing again. It was a nice day and sunny and warm, so it dried in no time. It was also an opportunity for Gareth to work on the truck, change the oil, rotate the tyres to ensure even wear, check the mechanical parts for wear, and do whatever other jobs might need doing. Kim would be busy checking our schedule and making the necessary bookings for the next few days.

We were back on the road shortly after dawn. We were going through rolling, fertile farmland and past rows and rows of hot houses, some derelict but others growing flowers. Kenya's chief exports include horticultural products, including flowers and tea. In 2005, the combined value of these commodities was USD 1,150 million, about 10 times the value of Kenya's next most valuable export, coffee.

The country has recorded huge growth in volume and value of cut flowers exported every year, from 120,220 tons in 2010 to 136,601 tons in 2014 to 159,961 tons in 2017, according to the Horticultural Crop Directorate. The floriculture industry earned USD 823 million. Kenya is the leading exporter of roses to the European Union, with a market share of about 38%. Approximately 50% of all exported flowers are sold through the Dutch Auctions in Aalsmeer, Holland, which is the largest building by footprint in the world, covering 51 hectares. The Boeing Everett factory is the largest building in the world by usable volume, but its footprint is only 40 hectares. Another 25% of production is delivered directly to customers, such as chains of supermarkets.

Floriculture in Kenya provides more than 100,000 direct jobs and supports two million indirect jobs. Kenyan flowers are sold in more than 60 countries. The success of the industry is based on active government support, mainly by facilitating trade through the provision of incentives in the form of nil or reduced duties and other taxes on imported raw materials crucial to the sector, such as greenhouses, greenhouse covers, shade netting, and refrigeration equipment for cooling and cold stores. The climate is favourable for flower production, and there is a hardworking, highly educated, and qualified workforce comprising both men and women.

Kenya receives a lot of tourists and is an airline hub in east and central Africa, so its large number of international destinations provides the essential air cargo capacity to get produce to market. Producers are keen to promote their adherence to high standards of production through compliance with codes of practice, traceability, due diligence, and ethical trading, which is what many First World Economy customers demand. However, there are still some companies that overinvest or invest in the wrong product, and the ongoing effects of the 2008 financial crisis, hence the many derelict greenhouses.

We stopped in the town of Naivasha for the next two cook groups to get whatever they needed, and as we had been here before, we knew our way around the centre, and we were soon back on the road. Our next stop was for lunch at Unilever's Chagaik Arboretum, located 10 kilometres outside Kericho, which is surrounded by its tea estate.

The estate has 11,000 hectares of tea gardens and employs 18,000 full-time and 4,000 seasonal workers. In order to get that lovely bag of tea that you drop into the cup in the morning, workers have to move through the hectares of tea gardens and pull off the top three new leaves from the bushes every two weeks. Then the harvested leaves are taken to the factory to be processed, usually fermented, and then dried for black tea or just dried for green tea. The tea is then packed into chests and taken to Mombasa, on the coast, to be auctioned.

Manufacturers buy in bulk and mix the different grades according to the particular product they are making. Tea used to be bought by consumers loose, and the first modern tea bags were only patented as late as 1903 and first appeared commercially the following year. The first tea bag packing machine was invented in 1929 by Adolf Rambold for the German company Teekanne, which still exists and produces 7.5 billion teabags a year. The heat-sealed paper fibre tea bag was patented in 1930 by William Hermanson, and the modern rectangular tea bag was not invented until 1944. It is a common misconception that tea bags are made from paper, as they often include plastic or nylon for durability. Environmentalists are pushing for a change in the industry due to health and biodegradability issues to reduce the amount of plastic in the environment. So next time you go shopping for tea, check the material used for the teabag and buy only unbleached paper tea bags.

Workers are paid piece rates, 10 Kenyan shillings per kilo, and the exchange rate when I visited was about 100 shillings to one USD. It doesn't seem very well paid, but this is one of the jobs that locals strive to obtain. Other benefits of employment here are that they also get free accommodation with water and electricity for the worker plus up to five members of his family, free education, for the children and free medical care. These are good jobs, and the pay is above the statutory minimum and is sought after.

We moved on to reach Kisumu in the late afternoon, which is a town sitting on the shores of Lake Victoria at the head of a bay. We weren't staying in the city but meandered our way through the suburbs to reach our campsite at Hippo Point, overlooking the bay. There was a clue in the name. There were hippos in the water, and we were warned to stay away from the shore, especially at night. That would not be a problem, as England were playing in the World Cup that night, and we would all be at the bar to watch the match that England won. The only problem would be getting back from the bar to the tent in the dark.

But of greater concern was the fact that we were camping at lake level on grass, and hippopotamus feed on grass at night. Our last camp had a fence between the lake shore and the camp, but there was no fence here. We would be safe in our tents, but the manager warned us to take a moment to check the area for hippopotamus before leaving your tent and to check when leaving the bar to get back to your tent. Before the match started, we had seen hippopotamus in the water, working their way along the shore looking for somewhere to come ashore and feed.

There were more safety instructions, and I wondered what you were meant to do if you check, for hippopotamus and there happened to be one there. The answer from the bar staff was that whatever happens, don't run, as he will charge. Stand still for a moment, and when the hippopotamus has seen you and is not charged whilst it is trying to assess whether you are in danger or not, back off slowly, facing it but not looking at it in the eye. I wasn't sure that I would want to stand still with a tonne of hippopotamus with attitude as it stood grazing near me. And something that only struck me later was, what happens if he sees you and then charges? They are the most dangerous animals in Africa and kill more people than any other animal.

There was a night guard who had a dual purpose. He had two seats, and he alternated between the two. One seat was just inside the gate to the campsite to check people in or out. His other seat was on a slight rise, overlooking the campsite and the shore. If he saw a hippopotamus on land and heard a tent zipper being opened, he would call out for you to stay inside. There was hippopotamus about, and since they made a noise, they had woken me up. I was now alert and wide awake and listening for any noise. The more I listened and thought about the warnings about going to the toilet in the dark, the more I needed to go.

I waited until the noise of animals pulling up and munching grass receded, and then I waited a little longer, and it seemed like an age to wait. With any noise that I heard, I was trying to interpret and guess whether it was a quiet hippopotamus working its way through some grass or whether it was some other nocturnal mammal rummaging around in the leaf litter under bushes. And how can I tell the difference between a quiet hippopotamus and some other animal in the dark from the noises that it makes?

I had not been on that particular training course, and my guidebook had not been specific on the matter. By now, I had had too much time to think about everything and whether I actually needed to go to the toilet or not, I now just had to go before I would ever get any more sleep. I put some clothes on for decency and opened my tent zip, moving the zip up and down several times to make sure that the guard had heard it and would warn me if there was a hippopotamus nearby.

There was no shouted warning, and so I walked to the facilities. My route took me past the guard's seat on the slight rise, and there was no one there. When I went around the corner and could see the gate, he was not at his other post by the gate. I had relied on him being there to do his job, and he was somewhere else. So, I was just lucky that I had avoided a fatal nocturnal encounter with a hippopotamus, but no thanks to the security guard.

The other problem about the still waters of the lake and the low-lying areas around the edge of the lake is that they are breeding grounds for mosquitoes. There were so many that, despite the warmth of the evening, I put on socks, long trousers, and a long sleeve shirt, plus loads of DEET on exposed skin, hands, face, and neck, which was the first time that I had used it since leaving Cape Town ten weeks ago. Mosquitoes were one of the reasons that Africa was not on my bucket list, but then again, I was seeing a lot of wildlife.

We left and set off for the border. It was a one stop border, with everything under one roof. It should be relatively straightforward, and my visa covered Tanzania, Uganda, and Rwanda. But I had to get my photo and my fingerprints taken to get into Uganda.

Then we were in Uganda. We passed through an area outside Jinja that was some sugar cane plantation for as far as the eye could see. Then we were in Jinja itself. We would be staying at the Nile River Expeditions Base Camp, overlooking the Nile just downstream of the dam at Jinja. We arrived in the afternoon and had time to do some laundry and go shopping, followed by an introduction to the various activities available and for us to make our preferences. We would be moving on the next day but returning in a few days' time. So, we booked up activities for later, but we had other things to do before we returned to Jinja.

We had a leisurely breakfast and time to do a few jobs or just go for a walk before we left the camp site and Jinja at 10am. Some cook groups had shopped the night before, others went off early in the morning to get stuff before leaving for the short journey to Kampala, the capital of Uganda.

The name of the country comes from the largest former kingdom in the south of the country, Buganda. Arab traders moved inland from the coast of East Africa in the 1830s. They were followed in the 1860s by British explorers searching for the source of the Nile. A group of 151 British Anglican missionaries arrived in the kingdom of Buganda in 1877 and were followed by French Catholic missionaries in 1879.

The British government chartered the Imperial British East Africa Company (IBEAC) to negotiate trade agreements in the region beginning in 1888. Before they had even started to negotiate any trade or treaties, there were a series of religious conflicts in Buganda, initially between Muslims and Christians and then, from 1890, between Anglican Protestants and French converted Catholics. Because of the civil unrest, the cost of trying to build trade routes with a lack of security and heavy financial burdens, caused IBEAC to claim that it was unable to meet its obligations in the region.

British commercial interests were adamant that they would protect the trade route to the Nile, which prompted the British government to annex Buganda and adjoining territories to create the Uganda Protectorate in 1894. Uganda became a British colony in 1905, and the capital was moved to Entebbe. The country became independent in 1962 and became a republic under President Milton Obote in 1963, and the capital was moved back to Kampala.

There is a large dam at Jinja that produces hydroelectric power. It is forbidden to take photos of either the dam or the bridge just upstream, so despite a great opportunity for photos of a grand piece of engineering, I could only look out of the window. Jinja is also the source of the Nile.

After leaving the urban sprawl, we were again driving through vast fields of sugar plantations stretching away as far as the eye could see. Kakira Sugar Works is the largest producer of sugar in Uganda, whose main plant is located in Kakira, 16 kilometres northeast of Jinja, producing 180,000 tons annually, or over 45% of national production. The second-largest producer is Kinyara Sugar Works located 200 kilometres northwest of Kampala near Masindi, not far from Lake Albert. Its annual production is 120,000 tons, or 30% of national output.

During the journey, Gareth slowed and hooted his horn a few times. It wasn't a warning to other traffic, animals on the road, or road rage; it was his way of telling us that there was something to see. We leapt up and looked out the windows. There was a large sign indicating that we were crossing the equator. This isn't the large tourist attraction that people go to see, but just a sign.

Halfway between Jinja and Kampala, we stopped at a well-known truck stop. This was Gareth's favourite meat on a stick market in Africa. You know that you are there when you see smoke from the barbecues drifting across the road. As any vehicle draws up, traders clutching beef or chicken on skewers rush towards it and grab on to door handles or open windows to be the first to get the sale.

There are also cold soft drink sellers, people holding pineapples and bananas for sale, and hawkers with their wares hanging from one arm. It is a hive of activity, as whenever another vehicle pulls up, the traders rush to be the first to trade with potential new customers. There are also Rolex sellers—not the watches, but chapattis covered with omelettes and then rolled up—a traditional street food in Uganda.

Chapter 12
Gorillas in the Mist

If more Africans had eaten more missionaries, the continent would be in better shape.
Maya Angelou

One who causes misfortune also teaches them wisdom.
African proverb

After checking out the market, we got back onto the road to brave the Kampala traffic to get to our next designated camp site at the Red Chilli Hideaway. It is a large, purpose-built hostel with some great reviews, and it certainly lived up to its name. It has carefully manicured and large gardens, a large, clean swimming pool, upgrades available, shot water in the showers, a competitively priced bar and restaurant, and a free shuttle to the local mall. It was a great place, and it was hidden away down a back street, and it was painted cream and magenta, not quite red but close enough.

There are several must-see sights to see in the city. Idi Amin's torture chamber. He joined the British Colonial Army and saw action against Somali rebels and against Mau. He rose through the ranks to become a major general in the Ugandan army. Aware that Ugandan President Milton Obote was planning to arrest him for misappropriating army funds, Amin launched a military coup in 1971 and declared himself president.

He was in power from 1971 to 1979, and his rule gained notoriety for its sheer brutality and oppressiveness. His time in power was characterised by rampant human rights abuses, political repression, ethnic persecution, extrajudicial killings, nepotism, corruption, and gross economic mismanagement.

In 1972, he exiled 60,000 Asians, half of whom immigrated to the UK. Amin expropriated businesses and properties belonging to the Asians and the Europeans who also fled and handed them over to his supporters. Businesses were mismanaged, and industries collapsed from mismanagement and a lack of maintenance or investment. This proved disastrous for the already declining economy and was a dark period in the country's history.

The number of people killed as a result of his regime is estimated by international observers and human rights groups to range from 100,000 to 500,000. Growing dissent against his persecution of certain ethnic groups and political dissidents meant that there were increasing numbers of members of all sorts of groups that faced persecution, such as religious leaders, journalists, artists, bureaucrats, judges, lawyers, students and intellectuals, criminal suspects, foreign nationals, and anyone who might be a threat.

There were also external issues, such as Uganda's very poor international standing due to Amin's support for the terrorist hijackers in Operation Entebbe, which led to more internal unrest and international isolation, except for some of his supporters, such as Libya. When Amin attempted to annex Tanzania's Kagera region in 1978, Tanzanian President Julius Nyerere had his troops invade Uganda. They captured Kampala and ousted Amin from power. Amin then went into exile, first in Libya and then in Saudi Arabia, and Uganda was left to pick up the pieces and rebuild the economy.

There were other activities on offer, such as a guided city walk, various museums, a boat trip on the lake, a chimpanzee sanctuary, plus lots of opportunities to go gorilla trekking or go on safari, but we would be going gorilla trekking in Rwanda, and we had been on many safaris to date, so these were of less interest to some in the group.

I spent the afternoon sitting in the sun and taking a few dips in the pool. Some people sat at the bar, and there was a game of Monopoly being played at one of the tables near the pool. Hazel had been into town with Mike, but she had twisted her ankle and had a big bandage around her ankle. She had crutches, but movement was difficult, and she was not sufficiently mobile to continue the trip. We would be moving on but will return via Kampala in a few days' time. Therefore, she would stay at the hostel until we came back through Kampala, and she would reassess the situation then.

Heather, David, Mike, Noodles, and Kristin had booked a tour to go and see some chimpanzees and would meet up with us again in a couple of days. Noah was off to do his own thing to get visas for Libya and Russia but planned to rejoin us. Hazel would be resting in the Red Chilli Pepper Hideaway to recuperate, so we made sure that she had everything that she needed until we passed back through Kampala.

It was therefore a much smaller group in the back of the truck, and we had plenty of space to spread out. Cook group shopping was a lot easier as the vegan and the strict vegetarian had left us for a few days. Therefore, I bought some meat for the meat eaters and those that don't eat fish and fish for the pescatarians. I got the fish, from the fishmonger, which had been caught that morning. We rarely had fish as we didn't have a fridge, and fish can go off quickly in hot climates. We kept food chilled by having a large, insulated box that we filled with ice, but just finding ice can be difficult. But I was cooking that evening, and I had found some ice to keep both the meat and the fish cool until the evening.

I could have bought the whole fish, but I asked for the fish to be filleted and the fishmonger shouted at her young assistant. The young lad did an expert job of descaling, decapitating, deskinning, gutting, and then filleting the fish. The husband turned up and started to chat. He had studied computer technology in England, studying and living not more than half an hour away from where I used to live, so we reminisced about long forgotten haunts. He had fled Uganda with his parents during the Amin years, hence his English education, but he missed his extended family, so after a few years, he had come back to marry a local and set up his fish selling business.

We crossed the equator on the main road. There was a lot more to see here than on our earlier crossing. There were lots of souvenir stands, cafes, restaurants, and hawkers. We stopped at a cafe where all the profits go to support a local orphanage. I took de rigueur photos of the white line painted across the road to indicate the equator, which passed through an arch made of a pair of artificial crossed elephant tusks and served as the entrance to a restaurant.

Then it was an afternoon drive to our bush camp, which was owned by Booth. Sometime ago, an overlanding truck stopped here, and there was nothing, but some subsistence crops, and the owner lived with his parents in the local village. Then there was a single house. Oasis Overlanding sponsored the eldest child to study in Kampala and, therefore, eventually to be able to support the rest of his family. Now there are three houses in the vicinity, and the farm has expanded.

We had a stop at the Lake Museum, which was a cafe, museum, and hostel. We bought some takeaway coffees in return for them letting us use their toilet facilities. We were going into some foothills and eventually into some stunning scenery. The road climbed into mountains, and into Kabale, which is one of the most scenic routes in East Africa, as we made our way to the very southwestern tip of the country. Kabale lies in a valley, but it is at an elevation of over 2, 000 metres above sea level.

After Kabale, we went up into the hills and over a pass on a dirt track road to reach our destination, a camp site overlooking Lake Bunyonyi. One of the islands in the lake is called Akampene Island, or Punishment Island. The local Bakiga tribe would leave unmarried pregnant girls on the island to starve or drown whilst trying to swim away from the island (as swimming skills are rare amongst Africans) as a warning to others. Unmarried men without the requisite cows to pay the dowry for a bride could visit the island and pick up one of the girls as a 'free' wife.

The camp was spread across some rising land overlooking the lake. The reception, bar, restaurant, and facilities were at one end of the site, and there were several paths running parallel to the shore to give access to various cabins. At the far end was a grassy area on a slope, but there was competition for pitches as there were only a few flat spaces. We ended up being quite spread out through the gardens on any flat space available. I had pitched my tent on a piece of flat grass just a metre from the shore of the lake. It was only later that I thought about crocodiles and hippopotamus, but soon I discounted the danger as I was aware of the procedures to be vigilant and exercise care. There was a thatched communal area with open sides that looked out across the lake, and a barbecue pit.

We had an opportunity to visit an orphanage run by Edison. It is located on the far side of the lake, and a boat came to pick us up and our overnight bags to take us across. We were shown around and then treated to a traditional evening meal. Our overnight stay helped provide some additional income to run the orphanage. There are many orphans in the country, as parents are affected by AIDS or HIV, become seriously ill, and are unable to cope with their children. Some children go to live with other family members, but many are still orphaned. Over 7% of the general population has AIDS or HIV, which is bad but not the worst countries, which are South Africa and Botswana, where infection rates are over 15%. The epidemic has decreased average lifespans by more than 20 years.

I was up at 4.30am and helped Kim, who was making packed lunches. It was still dark, and there was just a little light from the stars. There was a mist across the lake, and it obscured the tops of the hills around us. I lit a fire and boiled some water for the first brew of the day and to heat up some Rolexes that were to be our breakfast. We were being picked up by three minivans to be taken for the two-hour drive to Bwindi Impenetrable National Park to go on our gorilla trek. My driver introduced himself as Herbert.

One of our vans was going to another gate, but the other two minivans travelled in convoy to the main gate. We had an orientation talk given by Medi, one of the senior rangers, about the conservation and research work that they do here and some safety instruction. Then we split into smaller groups to meet our guides, guards, trackers, and researchers. The sun was trying its best to warm up the atmosphere, but at this elevation, it was still cool, and there were still patches of mist in the sheltered valleys.

We got into some Jeeps and drove down the road a couple of kilometres. We got out and started up a track into the forest with an armed guard and one guide, John, also dressed in khaki, at the front, another armed guard and another guide, James, and a researcher at the back.

Whilst we were having our peep talk, the trackers had returned to the gorilla family. Our group was going to visit the Bitukura group of gorillas. Originally, it was led by Ndahura, the brother of Rukuma. His brother fell out of a tree and died, and hence Rukuma was able to take over, but he is now the oldest member of the family, an elderly male with a distinctive bent finger. His name translates as Finger, as he seems to be giving everyone the one-finger salute. But he too has been usurped, and therefore the much stronger and younger male Mugisha is now the dominant male. His name means Lucky. There are four females, five adolescents, and some juveniles and baby gorillas.

We trekked into the jungle along a path, and then our lead guide left the trail and started hacking at the jungle with his machete. We met up again with our trackers, who were nearby the family group that was visiting. Trackers follow the family so they know where they are and report any unauthorised visitors or the presence of poachers. They track the gorillas as they move through the forest grazing, taking notes but also reporting back on their position, which is why it was so easy for us to find the gorillas. It really is an impenetrable forest, as the vegetation grows so thick and tall. Without a tracker, it would take ages to struggle through the forest and not see anything.

The gorilla family usually finishes eating in the late afternoon and will slow down to relax, make a nest, and settle down for the night. The trackers know where the animals are in the evening and will return in the morning to the nests and pick up the trail from there.

Our first sighting of tracks was where the animals slept for the night—a large, flat area with a few palm fronds or broad leaves for comfort. Their diet is also largely fibrous with plants, and their first morning activity is to get up and have a poo. Nearby every nest was a big pile of poo, lots of partly digested fibres similar to elephant poo but elephant poo, but is round, these really are just piles.

It's called the impenetrable forest as the steep mountain sides are covered with thick vegetation, and moving is a challenge. Even for the gorillas, if they make a few bad choices, they might slip down the hillside if they misplace a foot. Some of the gorillas climbed up the thinner trees to get to the best leaves, but the trunk couldn't support their weight, and the sapling would bend and break to deposit the gorilla on the floor, perhaps bruised but usually unharmed. And it was easy to see how Ndahura fell out of a tree and had a bad fall, which killed him.

The group would move off into the forest, and we would do our best to follow, but sometimes we would lose sight of them before picking up their trail again. Once they obligingly stopped, the forest was a little thinner, and sunlight reached the floor of the jungle. There were also some young saplings, and the gorillas bent over the thin trunk and picked at the new shoots at the top of the tree. Then they resumed; they wandered through the forest, but we were between them and where they wanted to go. The gorillas walked up to us, and we were told to stand still and upright and keep our hands by our sides. The gorillas didn't batter their eyelids but just walked right between us. It really was a close encounter.

We had our time with the gorillas, but it was time to leave them and return to the ranger station. We followed John out of the jungle, and we were one of the last groups to return. We had been promised an hour with the gorillas, but it was such a large family group that it was spread over quite a large area as they grazed in the forest that we had spent more than two hours watching the gorillas.

We got back to the road and walked up it back to the ranger station. It was late, and some of the other groups had had their hour and had returned and gone home. We ate our packed lunches and got back into the minivan to make our way out of the Bwindi Impenetrable Forest back down the valley through some spectacular scenery back to Lake Bunyonyi.

The rest of the afternoon was free to do as we liked—to sit at the bar or read or do laundry before the evening barbecue. Despite Uganda being a hot country, it was only when someone mentioned it that, at Lake Bunyonyi, we had not been pestered by mosquitoes. It is high up in the mountains and too cold at night for mosquitoes. The usual rule of thumb is that however hot it might be during the day; you don't find mosquitoes above an elevation of 1,500 metres, as it is too cold at night.

We left Lake Bunyonyi and crossed the border into Rwanda. We already had our East African visa, which covered entry into Kenya, Uganda, and Rwanda, but we still had to queue to get officially stamped out of Uganda and into Rwanda. It was a beautiful scenic drive through more mountains with jungle on the slopes and deep valleys with flat bottoms that were ideal for agriculture, all the way from the border to Kigali.

Rwanda is the fourth smallest country on mainland Africa, about two thirds the size of Switzerland or the same size as Albania. The area was dominated in the mid-eighteenth century by the kingdom of Rwanda, with Tutsi kings imposing anti-Hutu policies. The area was colonised by Germany in 1884 as part of Germany's East Africa, as confirmed by the Berlin Conference. During the First World War, this area was liberated from being a German colony by Belgium troops, advancing from the Congo in 1916. However, both countries continued to support the existing Tutsi-dominated hierarchy to govern the country.

In 1936, Belgium introduced a new identity card on which it would state whether the person was a Hutu or Tutsi, thus identifying divisions within society. In the 1959 Rwandan Revolution, Hutu activists began killing Tutsi and destroying their houses, forcing more than 100,000 people to seek refuge in neighbouring countries. Between 1934 and 1989, the population increased from 1.6 million to 7.1 million, putting immense pressure on land and food production for the increasing population.

In 1973, Juvénal Habyarimana took power in a military coup, but Hutu government discrimination against Tutsi continued. He managed to stay in power for nearly two decades, but in 1990, the Rwandan Patriotic Front, a rebel group composed of nearly 500,000 Tutsi refugees, invaded northern Rwanda from their bases in Uganda, initiating the Rwandan Civil War. However, neither side was able to gain a decisive advantage in the war, but by 1992, it had weakened Habyarimana's authority, and popular mass demonstrations forced him into a coalition with the domestic opposition and a ceasefire.

The ceasefire ended on 6th April 1994 when Habyarimana's plane was shot down near Kigali Airport, killing him and serving as the catalyst for the Rwandan genocide, which began within a few hours. Over the course of approximately 100 days, around 800,000 Tutsi and politically moderate Hutu were killed in well-planned and coordinated attacks.

The Tutsi-dominated RPF restarted their offensive and took control of the country methodically, gaining control of the whole country by mid-July and ending the genocide, but by then, two million Hutu had fled to neighbouring countries, fearing reprisals. There were United Nations troops in the country, but through political indifference, they were under resourced, undermanned and unable to interfere in the atrocities occurring, even if they were happening right in front of them. It is a beautiful country, but it is hounded by a disturbing history.

Our first stop in the country was in the capital, Kigali, at the Kigali Genocide Memorial. When Germany decided in 1907 to separate the administration of Rwanda from that of Burundi, they appointed explorer Richard Kandt as the country's first resident. He founded the city of Kigali in 1907 due to its central location in the country. He built a European style house in the city, which today is the Kandt House Museum of Natural History.

We parked in the car park of the Kigali Genocide Memorial and walked up to the entrance of the museum. It has exhibits of the Rwandan genocide in graphic detail, so it is not for the faint-hearted or sensitive. There are also details of other genocides, such as the Holocaust of the Jews in Germany and the Bosnian genocide, but there was no mention of the Armenian genocide by the Ottomans in 1915 or the genocide of the Herero in 1904-07 in Namibia, but then space is limited.

Driving about the city, I was surprised to see many modern, tall buildings with many company names and logos that I recognised. There was a lot of greenery, neatly mowed grass, and tree lined avenues. There were gardeners and road sweepers at work, and the city prides itself on being a clean, modern, and well organised city.

And there were nice cars on the streets, and there was a busy rush hour in the morning and evening. There are quite a few hills, so any journey will include several ups and downs that you would notice if you were walking or cycling but not in a car. I wasn't sure what to expect before I arrived, but what I saw was not what I would have expected to see in a month of Sundays.

Gareth dropped us off at the Discover Rwanda Hostel, not far from the city centre. There were several activities on offer, but many of them were gorilla trekking and safaris to see elephants, monkeys, or chimpanzees, which for those tourists that had just a week or two in the country would be a great opportunity, but for overlanders like us who had already seen all these things, they weren't that appealing, especially given the cost.

My immediate concerns were things like doing my laundry, getting a haircut and chilling. It might seem that I do a lot of laundry, but I am not obsessive. It's a hot climate, so you sweat a lot, you use a lot of DEET to keep insects away, the roads are dusty, we camp a lot, and when you are living out of a rucksack, even freshly cleaned clothes put away in the rucksack rub against dirty clothes and are not that fresh when you go to put them on. Laundry is also often just a hand wash or a rinse in the shower, which is never as good as a machine wash, but I would use a machine periodically as and when the opportunity arose.

That evening, I walked up the road to a restaurant advertising African food called Ingeniously African Bites. It was empty inside and served a buffet style evening meal. There were large cauldrons with small fires underneath each one to keep them warm. There was rice, potato, banana soup, beef stew, and a chicken stew. And nothing else. No green vegetables, no fruit, no fish, and whilst they had beer, they had no wine. I walked out and tried another restaurant.

I tried the Poivre Noire, offering French cuisine. They had plenty of starters, but just three main courses, and none of them were fish, and it seemed expensive. I tried another restaurant with another poor result. On the off chance, I walked into a restaurant, and without looking at the menu, I asked the maitre'd whether they had fish available and whether they had white wine. He was all charmed and said yes to both, so I found my preferred evening restaurant.

I sat down, ordered Captain Fillet and a white wine from the waitress, and waited. There were thirty or forty tables, but just me at one, and, as I looked around, I saw Kim and Gareth at another and a large space void of people. Gareth and Kim would have the experience of other drivers and travellers, so they would always know the best place to go, but I had just stumbled on it by luck. I could always ask them for the best place to go, but travelling also includes finding things out for yourself. I could read the country guide to discover the best places to eat, but then I might be robbed of having an experience.

We exchanged greetings, but I didn't want to spoil a romantic evening for two, so I chose to sit by myself. The waitress came back and said that my first choice of wine wasn't available, so I chose another. She was back in a few minutes to apologise and to say that my second choice wasn't available. I ended up with a glass of house white. I asked for a bottle, but she said that it comes in a box and is only available in glass. Wine snobs turn their noses up at wines in a box, and some also give a withering stare at the thought of plastic corks. That was the first time that I had ever been told that a wine in a restaurant comes out of a box, although I had suspected it for years.

The next day, I went shopping with the rest of the cook group in the centre of the city. I ordered a taxi from the hostel to take us from the hostel to the centre of the city to go shopping for the evening meal. The taxi driver called Sam was chatty and talked all the way to our destination. As we drove past the Hotel des Mille Collines, the hotel featured in the award-winning film Hotel Rwanda, where Paul Rusesabagina saved 1,200 from genocide by providing them with a sanctuary within the hotel of which he was the manager.

We passed the Presidents Palace, currently occupied by Paul Kagame, right next door to the national bank, and we joked about it, with him being next to the bank so that he could fill his wallet whenever he wanted to, and in the event of a coup, he was near the money. He was born a Tutsi and led the Rwanda Patriotic Forces, which liberated the country and ended the genocide. He has been in power since 2000 (although he was vice president for the period 1994-2000). He has been re-elected several times, but each time his re-election was preceded by a change to the constitution to allow him to stand again.

We left Kagali to drive into the hills and reach Musanze. It was a very scenic drive through some stunning scenery. The road climbed out of Kagali at an elevation of 1,567 metres to cross several passes. There were soaring mountains and plunging valleys with steep sides as the road snaked its way diagonally across the valley sides. The fields stretched up the sides of the valleys at almost impossible angles and completely filled the bottoms of the valleys. It was the second most stunning scenic drive in East Africa.

Then we arrived in Musanze and drove up the road from the centre to the Catholic Community Pastoral Centre of Notre Dame de Fatima, which sits at the top of the hill. We drove through the gates into the compound and were met by Herbert, the same guide and driver who had taken a group of us from Lake Bunyonyi to see the gorillas in Bwindi Impenetrable Forest.

There was Golden Monkey Trekking, an opportunity to go for a walk and hopefully see some rare and endangered species of monkey, only found in the

Virunga Mountains. They live in social groups of 80-100 led by a dominant male. There are two groups of habituated monkeys, and just as with the gorillas, you are allowed to spend just one hour with them.

The hike up Mount Bisoke, guided by a ranger, sits on the border between Rwanda and the Democratic Republic of Congo, whose summit is 3,711 metres and takes half a day to reach a summit. It is an extinct volcano with a lake in the crater created as the East African Rift Valley slowly expands and magma wells up between the two tectonic plates as they part company.

It is in these mountains where the Dian Fossey site is located, between Mt Bisoke and Mt Karisimbi, at an elevation of over 3,000 metres in the Volcanoes National Park and Virunga National Park. The site was abandoned during the troubles in the 1990s and is now derelict. Dian Fossey was murdered in 1985 and buried nearby, next to her favourite gorilla, Digit, and several other gorilla burial sites. The Dian Fossey Memorial Fund continues to monitor 10 of the 15 guerilla groups in the area.

There was an opportunity to visit Iby'iwacu, now a living cultural village, but formerly the inhabitants were poachers who have now embraced a new way of life and contribute to the conservation efforts in the mountains. They also show their former hunting skills with bows and arrows, how they hunted, the witch doctor and the medicines that they obtained from the forest, traditional dances, and how they subsisted in the forest.

Near the border with Uganda is another volcano, Muhabura. There are also the twin lakes of Burera and Ruhondo. This was originally one lake, but Mt Sabinyo erupted, and a lava flow cut the lake in half. Our lunch was in a local village, and we were served a traditional meal accompanied by a glass of banana beer. There are souvenir stands and an opportunity to watch the women weave clothes, visit their homes, and watch them create local handicraft items before having some relaxation in a dugout canoe and being paddled along the lake shore.

There are caves that host huge colonies of bats that roost there every night. More than 20 kilometres of caves, many of which can be explored. They were used as ancient ancestral shelters, but there is some darker, more recent history when they were used as shelters during the genocide. People had escaped towns and villages to seek shelter in the caves from the roving bands of murderers. However, those people sheltering there were discovered and massacred.

Lake Kivu sits on the border between Rwanda and the DRC Congo and is one of the great lakes of the African Rift Valley, with gorgeous beaches and a hot water spring at Gisenyi. The lake has a large population of fish, which fishermen exploit to sell in local markets. At the lake's bottom, there are more than an estimated 55 billion cubic metres of methane. The Ruzizi River flows out of the lake into Lake Tanganyika. In the distance, just visible through the clouds, is the dark form of the Nyiragongo volcano, which destroyed the town of Goma in 2002.

Chapter 13
Nile River Horse Rides

African leaders should not turn the continent into a giant collector of donations and loans from wealthy nations; they must find some other plausible means to help establish their economic security so as to minimise poverty. This incoherent blunder must be scrutinised.
Dup Chak Wuol

Do not tell the man who is carrying you that he stinks.
African proverb

I spent the morning walking around the fabric market in Musanze, which, confusingly, is also called Ruhengeri. Several of us had tried to do this the day before but had failed to find it. In reality, and unbeknownst to us, it was a public holiday the day before, and many of the shops and the fabric market were shut. I had visited the right building, but there were only a few banks open, and the rest of the building was in darkness. I went with Sarah and Jacci to find the fabric market, and whilst we were sure we were in the right place, we couldn't see anything that looked like a market.

We were in a supermarket, and after buying what we needed, we asked the cashier for directions. We were in the right building, but the fabric market is on the third and fourth floors. We found the staircase and climbed up. The building was still quiet on the ground and first floors, but there was a lot of noise coming from the upper floors.

On the third floor was the fabric market, and we started to wander around. The system is that you find the material that you want and buy it from the stall holder, and then you go upstairs to the next level and approach one of the many seamstresses on the fourth floor to turn your chosen fabric into the garment of your choice.

Some of the seamstresses with no work will come down to the third floor and seek out potential customers. We were looking around, and Janine introduced herself to us and escorted us around the stalls.

I just love the huge array of African prints that are available. Despite the hundreds of stalls that are showing off their wares, I noticed very few repeats of patterns that I had already seen. I saw many patterns that I liked and could appreciate the artistry, but none that I could see that would become a favourite item of clothing.

The girls had chosen a number of fabrics, and eventually I saw one that was just me. We walked up the stairs to the fourth floor and handed over our fabrics to Janine. She took our measurements and our requirements, such as long sleeves, short, tight, or loose, trousers, fun pants, and the like. She noted everything done in chalk on her work bench and asked us to come back in three hours.

We went back to the Catholic Community Pastoral Centre of Notre Dame de Fatima, where we were staying, and had some lunch. I ordered a mushroom lasagna, but the girls and Noodles who had joined us ordered pizza. I had a lovely dish of mushroom lasagna, which was swamped with a thick cheese topping. However, the girls got their pizzas, and the dough was raw. They sent it back, and all the kitchen did was put the plate back into the oven. Therefore, when the pizzas were served for the second time, the now partially cooked dough was stuck to the plate and not very appetising.

Whilst we were having lunch, another overlanding truck came into the compound. Most of the drivers and guides know each other or have even worked together, and we often meet up with other trucks. Invariably, it was a chance to swap stories and have a party, which was what was planned for that evening.

After we had finished our lunch, we returned to the market. Noodles came with us to pick up her dress and skirt from a seamstress in the general market. She tried them on, and they were very flattering and were cut just right to great effect. Then we walked on to the fabric market to find Janine. In those three hours, she had created a top, a skirt, and two pairs of trousers. We were all delighted with our choices. On the way out of the market, both Sarah and I saw the ideal material at the same time. Sarah plays roller derby at home in Australia, and there on the stall near the exit and hanging up at the back of the stall was fabric with roller skates printed on it. She was overjoyed and had to stop to buy a length.

In the morning, we had a communal breakfast with the other truck. Some of them were complaining about a particular member of their group who seemed to do as little as possible to contribute to the jobs that the group had to do. The advertising and the joining instructions for the trip make it clear that it is camping, and despite having two drivers and guides, it is not their role to do all the jobs that need to be done. Guests are expected to contribute, and people are expected to join in with all the communal chores. But whatever the size of the group, there is always at least one who doesn't understand this, at best, or at worst, it's just too damn lazy to join in. I am appalled and outraged that someone can think that a particular rule doesn't apply to them and that they don't need to do any of the jobs.

I was sympathetic and empathetic as there was one person like that on our truck and there were only eight people in the group, but there was still one person who was a pain, full of himself, talked rubbish, didn't listen to any of his fellow travellers, didn't join in doing the jobs, thought the world of himself, and didn't pull his weight in getting any done. Five of the eight independently talked about this individual with vitriol, so it wasn't just one person's biased opinion. And to quote an often used saying, you can get on with most people most of the time, but it is rare that you can get on with all of the people all of the time, and some tolerance is needed. Sometimes you just get a feeling about a person, and before I had had any of these conversations, I had the feeling that he was not going to be someone that I would relate to.

I tried booking an air flight home, but it timed out. The internet was slow and fell over several times, but I tried again, and the flight was still very cheap, but whilst booking, the price doubled. I retried, but the cheap fare that had attracted me in the first place was still showing, but again, it was not available when I hit the buttons and the actual fare had increased from an advertised euro260 to an actual price of euro630. So in frustration, I decided to try booking another day in another town when the internet was a bit better.

After several days in the same place, it was time to move on and leave the Catholic Community Pastoral Centre of Notre Dame de Fatima in Musanze. I didn't have an alarm clock, and we were due to get up early for the drive to the border. Mike was in the next door tent, and I had asked him to make enough noise in the morning and to bang on the side of my tent to make sure that I was awake in time for breakfast and the departure.

I would not like to miss breakfast, and I hate to be rushed or to delay the group. Mike was as good as his word, and I was awake and dressed in plenty of time. But despite the amount of noise that Mike had made and that I added to as I packed away my sleeping bag and took down my tent, Kenny was late getting up, which wasn't unusual.

He had a habit of arriving late for breakfast, grabbing his food, and then taking down his tent. Then he would sit on the truck and eat his breakfast whilst the cook group and some helpers washed and packed away the breakfast things, and then we were ready to go. At which time he had just about finished his breakfast. His dirty plate would sit on the truck all day, dry hard, and attract flies. At the next camp site, someone would tidy up the truck and drop the dirty plate into the washing up bowl to be washed by the cook group, who had to scrub hard to get the dried food removed, which was always difficult and potentially unhealthy as we only had cold water to wash in when camping. He got away without ever helping to clear up after breakfast and do more work for everyone else. But we left on schedule.

It was a short, half-hour drive to get back to the border between Rwanda and Uganda. We had a good view of Mt Bisoke as we drove past. The mountain had been sheathed in clouds all the time that we had been in Musanze. This morning, as we were leaving, from the town side it was still covered in cloud, but from the east, where the early morning sun was shining directly on it, it was clear. It was clear enough to see the conical point and the shoulders of the cone volcano, but that was little consolation to those of us who had climbed up it in the fog along the wet, slippery paths and stood on the rim of the crater and could see nothing of the panoramic view as promised in the guidebook.

The scenery was even more stunning as we made our way towards Kampala. It would be a long journey, so we stopped at the same little farm that we had camped at earlier on our way to Rwanda, owned by Nbooth. I pitched the tent in exactly the same spot that I had pitched it the last time that we were here. We lit the fire and started the evening meal. Several children came over to play with us and watch us cook and eat. The other kids left, but Nbooth's own brood stayed with us, and we were happy for them to watch, answer their questions, and try some of our food until it was their bedtime.

It was a cold night, and there was heavy dew, so everything was damp. We were up and away on the road going back to Kampala the same way that we had driven to get from Kampala to Rwanda. We didn't stop in Kampala but drove through it. We were going to stop at the Red Chilli Hideaway, but Hazel was no better, and she had phoned to say that she was going home and would not be rejoining us.

We stopped once at a bus stop to pick up a couple of T shirts and fleeces that some of us had ordered in Jinja, and by arrangement, the screen printer agreed to meet us at this bus stop in Kampala. It was an unusual arrangement, but then again, this is Africa, and so many times had we found something unusual that we had even had an expression for it, this is Africa, shortened to TIA. I had my doubts about whether we would ever see the chap again since we had paid but he was true to his word and was waiting in the rain at the bus stop with the goods that had been ordered. We drove across the dam and on to our camp site, overlooking the Nile downstream from the dam.

Jinja is Uganda's adventure playground and is also the outflow of Lake Victoria, where the Nile begins its 6,700-kilometre journey to the sea. The scenery in this area is spectacular, and it is a superb place to go whitewater rafting or kayaking. There were other activities available, such as quad biking, horse riding, or a visit to a local education project. The camp site at Nile River Explorers Resort is set high on a bluff above the Nile. The Ninja dam is upstream, and there used to be whitewater rafting on the section of river below us. But with the building of the second ninja dam just downstream, the front of the camp is now a wide, slow-moving river before it widens again to be held back by the second dam completed in 2003.

Billy and Sime, who run the camp and the water sport activities, took us through the various options. There was boogie boarding, grade three and grade five rafting, and dual kayaking. Plus, there is potential for lessons for those that had not kayaked before. You could also hire stand up boards or sit on kayaks and mountain bikes. Plus, horse riding so there was something for anyone who might want to do some adrenaline sports. Some of us had already booked activities the last time that we were here, but it was an opportunity to reconsider and book something extra.

That night in the bar, the Russia v Spain World Cup match was being screened on television. I was not sure who I was supporting, as I have been on holiday and worked in both countries. The score was a draw at 1-1 after extra time, so it was a penalty shootout and the best of five. Spain lost by one penalty. I didn't hear any Russian being spoken at the bar, but there was a whole overlanding truck of Spanish speakers, and there was a collective groan when Spain's striker missed a penalty, and it was all over.

It was 1st July and Canada Day, so Noodles were celebrating. It was also the day that the Ugandan government introduced a social media tax. In order to get onto Facebook, WhatsApp, LinkedIn, Twitter, or any other social media platform you subscribe to, you had to pay the tax via Airtel Money, for which you needed a local phone. The internet speeds were already slow, and the imposition of a tax just made it harder and a less hospitable and inviting country. We had four more days here before crossing into Kenya, so none of us were about to rush out and get an Airtel Money phone to get a connection.

I went for a walk along the track that led to NRE Camp for some fresh air and to see how my leg was healing. I had somehow gained a hamstring injury, and just as it was getting better, I injured it again, so I had been taking it easy for a while, but I wanted to get back to doing activities and improving my level of fitness. My plan after finishing travelling northwards through the length of Africa was to go for a long walk and hire a horse for a long ride along El Camino, the pilgrim route across northern Spain to Santiago de Compostela, and finally onto the sea. I felt alright, so I went to reception to book a three-hour horse ride for the next day.

I was at reception talking to Billy and was about to book it up when he introduced me to Suze, who runs Nile River Horse Rides, who by chance had come in and was standing next to me. She was a former overland truck driver, and we had several mutual friends as she knew both Kim, Gareth, Grace, and Malcolm.

It rained at night. There were just a few spits, and I was snug in my sleeping bag, but I had left the fly sheet open. If it was just a few drops, it would be alright, but it got steadily heavier, so I had to get up and close the fly. It was just as well that I had gotten up, as there was some washing and drying on the roof of the tent, which I had forgotten about, so I rescued that as well. Some of it was what I was going to wear to go riding, so I needed it to be dry. My long trousers had been at the bottom of the locker, and I can't remember the last time that I had worn them, at least over two months ago when I had gone riding in Victoria Falls, and as it was summer, I was in shorts and sandals. They were creased and full of dust, as nowhere on the truck is free from the clouds of dust that get thrown up from the dirt tracks, so I had rinsed them through the evening before.

I had a leisurely breakfast, and people departed for their whitewater rafting, kayaking, or whatever other activity they had chosen to do. The stables were on the opposite bank, so I walked down the cliff face and got a water taxi to cross the river to the far bank. I checked with my taxi driver, Luka, that he would be waiting for me on the river below the stables at lunch time to take me back, and he promised that he would be there.

I climbed the bank, walked along the clifftop, and was greeted by Suze, who was waiting for me on the veranda of the main building. I was the only rider that morning, and I am an experienced rider, but I still had to have a briefing. Most of it was about the usual health and safety issues and a description of the ride. I requested no trotting as my leg felt fine, but I didn't want to overexert it; therefore, it would be walking and cantering.

The African influence on the briefing related to the villages that we would be passing through. The children would run towards us waving and shouting, so we would always walk through the villages, and if there were children, the lead guide would ask them not to get too close to the horses, and we would stop if they were too close.

Another problem would be the goats. These would be tied to a peg pushed into the ground, and the hazard would be if the peg was on one side of the track and the goat might be on the other side with the tether stretching across the track. So riders had to be careful around goats. My only question was about snakes and how the horses react to them. Some horses are skittish around snakes and anything that looks like a snake, such as rope or hosepipe. But these horses are not afraid of snakes, so that was one less problem.

I was introduced to my guides, the lead guide was George, and the back marker was Noah, and as per instructions, I would be riding between the two of them in a single file. I was also introduced to my horse, named Rusty, and it was clear that his coat had been the inspiration for his name. He was a strong, powerful horse, and I was advised that he had a marvellous character and was only too eager to canter, so I might have to hold him back when we go through a village.

We set off and headed away from the river. We crossed the single tarmac road, and then there were mud tracks through the village into the hills. We had several canters where the track was clear, but we walked through the villages.

George pointed out several plants, such as jackfruits, yams, and sweet potatoes, as we passed small fields around small huts. There were adults sitting in the shade in front of their homes and children playing in the yards. They all smiled and waved, and just as I had been warned, the children shouted and waved, and George kept telling them to stay away from the horses. George was a local lad, had worked at the stables for nearly twenty years, and knew most of the villagers by name.

The cantering was fine, but the walking was a little trouble. Just like humans, horses walk at different paces. George's horse had a faster walk than Rusty, and as the gap between us opened up, Rusty would break into a slow trot. I could rein him in, but as soon as he was walking and I relaxed, he would break into a trot again. Even if we were right behind George, Rusty would still be doing a slow trot to keep up with George. I purposefully didn't want to rise to the trot and strain my leg, so it was just uncomfortable to sit in a trot and continually rein him back into a walk. Eventually he settled down and walked, and when the gap was large enough, I would kick him into a canter to catch up, and then settled back into a walk.

Our route took us up into the hills, and we passed through huge sugar cane fields, probably growing sugar on behalf of the Ugandan Sugar Corporation. The cane was above head height, so it obscured the views. However, there were also tea plantations, and with the bushes less than waist height, we had some good views of the scenery beyond the tea gardens. We stopped on a slope with a good view of the river in the distance. Off to our left was the lower Jinja Dam, and in front of us was a large steel mill with a large pall of steam or smoke rising into the air and drifting off to the north.

Then it was time to return to the stables, and we followed the river upstream with some great views across the river to the far side. I got off the horse and thanked George and Noah. It was my first time on a horse since Victoria Falls nearly two months ago, and I had a hamstring injury that had held up remarkably well, so I was pleased. However, I was not riding fit, and it hurt to walk down the bank to find Luka and the boat to take me back across the river.

I gingerly climbed the steps up the cliff to the campsite and sat in the bar for the rest of the day. It was England v Colombia, so it was a very busy bar, and after extra time, it was still a 1-1 draw, so it was a nail-biting penalty shot out, which England won, but only just.

I slept well that night, but not for the whole night. There were two other overlanding trucks there. One was leaving at 4.30am, and the other one left at 6am. Therefore, there was a lot of noise of people packing away tents, talking, coughing, and heavy diesel engines throbbing away in the early morning. Plus, a few people who had celebrated football too vigorously the night before had to be woken up from a deep alcohol-induced slumber.

We said goodbye to Uganda and crossed into Kenya. Our yellow fever cards were checked and our temperature taken, and luckily, we all passed. Of the nearly 200 border crossing, that I have made over the last ten years, and yes, I record every date, country, and crossing as some visa request forms ask for all countries visited in the last ten years, I have found that border officials are usually surly, grumpy, and unsmiling, but these border guards were unusually chatty, and we exchanged stories about the football the night before and were asked what we thought England's chances were at winning. Everybody in Africa seems to follow an English team, and everybody was watching the World Cup.

In the late afternoon, we had to have an emergency stop as it suddenly started pouring and the sides were up, and unusually, the beach was open for the breeze, and several of us got really wet before we could pull off the road and cover the beach and put the sides down. It was 6pm when we arrived at Naiberi River Resort, put up the tents, and started cooking under an open sided structure next to our pitch.

It was a lovely campsite, popular with overlanding trucks, and it had a huge underground bar with an open fire and a stream running through the middle of the bar, but we were the only truck in camp that night, and we had the place virtually to ourselves. I played Monopoly with Jacci and Noodles in the bar and drank some whisky—not the ordinary stuff that you usually find in bars but Lagavulin 16-year-old single malt. It is unusual to find such a good whisky in an overlanding camp site bar, but either the barman knows his whisky or they have a regular that insists on this brand.

It was a late start but, no lie-in, as a lie-in when you are camping is not as nice as when you are tucked up in a comfy, warm bed. We were at an elevation of 2,360 metres, and it had been cold overnight. Also, there was an early morning mist, so whilst we drove through the central highlands, we didn't see very much, and it was cold and damp on the truck. It only cleared late in the morning when the sun burned off some of the clouds.

Chapter 14
Nakuru National Park

No other continent has suffered such a bizarre combination of foreign thievery and foreign goodwill.
Barbara Kingsolver

Revolutions are brought about by men who think as men of action and act as men of thought.
Sierra Leone proverb

We drove through Nakuru to the outskirts of the town to our campsite. The town is the fourth largest in Tanzania, was founded by the British during the colonial period, and lies at an elevation of 1,850 metres. The first and second presidents of Kenya, Jomo Kenyatta, and Daniel Arap Moi, maintained their semi-official residences within the city. For a long time, the city has been a hotbed of Kenyan politics and was home to a variety of colourful politicians, including the late Kariuki Chotara, Kihika Kimani, the late Mirugi Kariuki, and Koigi Wamwere.

The local economy is based on agriculture, manufacturing, and tourism. The city is surrounded by a vast, fertile area that grows coffee, wheat, barley, maize, beans, and potatoes. There are also dairy farms as well as arable farms. Large manufacturing plants include the Menengai soap factory, the Car & General Motorcycle plant, the Eveready Battery Plant, Fertiplant East Africa, and many others. The city is also the place where the country's four largest supermarket chains were founded, Nakumatt, Naivas, Tuskys, and Gilanis. For tourists, the big attraction is Lake Nakuru National Park, which surrounds Lake Nakuru just to the south of the city and is known for its wildlife but famous for its flamingos.

It was a bright, sunny afternoon, and we had time to do some jobs, but there was no internet. It is nice to get away from the internet, television, and phones, but it is also very useful for checking maps, reading up about the places we would be visiting, checking in with friends and family, and making bookings. It is surprising how much we rely on, it and take it for granted when we don't have it. The internet is fast, free, and everywhere at home but TIA.

We were going or an early morning safari in Nakuru National Park. We were picked up in three minivans, and my driver introduced himself as John. It was just ten minutes to the entrance, and we waited whilst forms were filled in to record who was visiting from which country and passport details before we were allowed through the gates. We had been on several safaris, but everyone is different, and you never know exactly what you might see.

Then we drove in and straight away saw zebras and Cape buffalo. We saw a white rhino as it browsed in the jungle. We caught glimpses of its huge horn and its back, but it mainly kept its head down. As it moved, we would drive along the road a little to try to get a better view, but there were always some trees or bushes between us that blocked a good view. Eventually, it turned away from the road and disappeared into the jungle.

There were small monkeys sitting in the trees and watching us as we went past. Further along the tracks through the park, we came across several troupes of baboons. We stopped for a while to watch them until they moved deeper into the jungle and away from the track.

Down by the lake shore, there were several trees sticking out of the water. In 2015, there was some plate tectonic activity and earthquakes, the result of which was that the water level in Lake Nakuru rose between two and three metres, as did several other lakes in the rift valley. The increase in the water level flooded the shorelines, so the lake is a bit bigger than it used to be.

We reached the end of Flamingo Road, and despite the name, it was a track, not a road, and found some of the park buildings that used to look out over the lake. Now their foundations and some of the brick work stand in the water. There was a pelican swimming through one of the buildings and a stork standing on the roof of another of the flooded abandoned buildings.

We saw a hippopotamus grazing out of the water. It was a cool and overcast morning, so it had left the protection of the water to eat some grass. We drove the length of the lake to see the flamingos. Lake Nakuru's waters are rich in blue-green algae and diatoms that flamingos feed on.

There was a track down to the old shoreline that had been flooded. The minivans parked where they could turn around, and we walked to the water's edge. When the lake level rose, many of the flamingos for which the lake was renowned moved to other lakes. Now that the water level has stabilised and the habitat is recovering, the numbers of flamingos are recovering. The grass is green and lush, and new wetlands are being created. There will be more ecosystem alterations as the former wetlands are now flooded, but the higher water levels will create new wetlands. Some trees have drowned and died, and others now have their roots in a higher water table and are struggling and will eventually die.

We saw Maribou storks, pelicans, and, of course, flamingos, but not the hundreds of thousands that this lake used to be renowned for. It is possible to see up to 400 species of birds according to the guidebook, and we positively identified pelicans, spoonbills, and yellow billed storks and saw many others that were not positively identified, only probable sightings. We drove on to see more Cape buffaloes, land warthogs and yet more zebras. We stopped for a break and a short walk to see the Makalia Falls, a two-tier fall with a short upper section and a long plunge into a near circular plunge pool. There is a camp site here, one of the few places that people can camp in a national park.

There are also black rhinoceros, which are protected here, but we didn't see any, but there were Bohor reedbuck, Defassa waterbuck and the endangered Rothschild giraffe. We drove past some ostriches to reach Nakuru Lodge. This is built on a hill overlooking the lake, with some great views. Games tend to rest in the middle of the day, so there is little point in driving around in the heat, so we had a two-hour rest. There was a bar, a restaurant, a swimming pool, and a souvenir shop.

We had eaten our packed lunches earlier in the day whilst we were at Makalia Falls, but some still ordered food. The bar was open, but several of us didn't want to spend two hours in the bar and then go on another drive around the park. Most of us had done several safari drives, so we opted to ask the driver to take us back to our camp site. Two thirds of the group wanted to see more, so they stayed at the lodge until later in the afternoon, when the game would have finished their siestas, and they would be moving again. Some of the group swapped seats so that the third van returned to the campsite early and we had the afternoon to ourselves.

Noah, Stefano, and Noodles were leaving us to take a taxi to Nairobi to fly to Ethiopia. Noodles needed to get a visa, as she didn't have one for Ethiopia.

Visas need to be obtained in the passport holder's own country and can't be bought at a land border, but they can be obtained on landing at an airport. Noah and Stefano were leaving to go and see the lava lake at Erta Ale in the Afar Depression, and all three would rejoin us when we arrived in Addis Ababa.

I wanted to see Erta Ale as well, but it had erupted the year before and there was little activity to see, so I planned to see it another time when there would be more rising lava to see. There are only four permanent lava-filled volcano craters in the world. The one in Antarctica is remote and difficult to reach. The one in Congo is fraught with difficulty due to a lack of security, insurgencies, and political instability. Only those in Ethiopia and Hawaii are more easily accessible, but both have erupted recently, so the lakes are low.

We stopped at a lookout over the rift valley on our way to Isiolo. We took a short cut of 18 kilometres, which would cut 80 kilometres off the distance had we continued along the main tarmac road around Mount Kenya National Park. But there was a catch, it was not a tarmac road, it was just a series of deep ruts, muddy in places, and bumpy. When a section got too badly churned up, drivers would drive around it, widening the track. Now the track was easily eight vehicles wide with impassable sections seemingly everywhere, so it was still getting wider, and I wondered whether the extra bends around the worst sections were making the short cut longer in both distance and time terms.

We reached Isiolo, a large town where we stopped to buy three days' worth of supplies, as northern Kenya is sparsely populated, and we were unsure whether there were any supermarkets or markets where we could buy supplies. We passed several large plastic greenhouses, which were now derelict. One of them was called Uhuru, named after Uhuru Peak, the highest summit on the rim of the Kibo volcanic cone, just one of three former volcanoes that created Mount Kilimanjaro. The flower industry is booming, but some companies collapsed after the 2008 financial crisis.

The scenery slowly changed from lush farmland and jungle to dry savannah, and for the first time on our trip northwards, we saw camels. We were following a main road with an excellent tarmac surface going north, and despite the quality of the road, it was quiet and had little traffic.

We turned off the road up a rough track to try to find a bush camp, but there was a homestead and a ranger who suggested that we move on down the road. We tried again with Gareth just driving off the road into savannah. We were lucky and eventually found a suitable spot. We had been on the road for several hours but there was still virtually no traffic on the road, so we didn't have a problem with road noise or being seen. But the downside was that just here, there were loads of crickets jumping about everywhere into your hair and drinks, surprising you when they land on your knee or hand.

I was woken up during the night by a noise, but I didn't know what it was. I listened for a while and heard a few noises somewhere behind my tent, but it didn't seem like a large animal, so I was not duly perturbed. But once I was awake, I felt like I needed a pee, not because I desperately wanted one, but because I had started to think about it, and so, whether I actually needed one or not, the only way I was going to get back to sleep was to go and have one.

I put my sandals on and unzipped the tent. I was walking towards a bush when I heard some rustling from it. I froze and listened. After a moment, there was some more rustling. I told myself that if it was a large predator, it would have already attacked, so I was safe, but I didn't necessarily believe myself. Logic and emotion are not strong bedfellows. I walked backwards, keeping my front to the rustling bush, until I was far enough away to turn around. I retraced my steps and found another bush that didn't rustle.

It was a 450 kilometres drive from Isiolo to the border, and we had three days to do it in and we had allowed ourselves so long as the roads were so poor. But unbeknownst to us, the road had been upgraded. There was now a long, flat, smooth ribbon of tarmac marching confidently across the savannah. There were white lines down the sides and yellow lines down the middle, dotted where you could overtake, and solid yellow on the bends and hills. There were crash barriers, new bridges, and crawler lanes up the longer, steeper hills. Therefore, we stuck to the schedule but just got up later, had a longer lunch break, and stopped earlier.

We passed a dead tree lying on the ground not far from the road, and Gareth slowed and stopped, then reversed so that we were alongside the tree. We had an unscheduled stop to cut up some wood and restock our fuel supplies. Out of nowhere, three women and two men appeared, offering us little trinkets to buy.

Despite being a long way from anywhere and seemingly with no human activity nearby, it was another TIA moment and a reminder that wherever you are, you are never alone in Africa. This was home to several nomadic tribes, like the Rendille in Marsabit and the Samburu (cousins of the Maasai), who still wear very distinctive and often elaborate traditional dress. Pink was a favourite and popular colour. Despite the march of progress, they still have a strong sense of tribal loyalty and cling to their traditional beliefs and culture.

Some way away from the road, but running parallel to it, was a row of pylons with cables running between them. But in Africa, TIA work had stopped on the pylons, and the cables were only strung from the pylons to somewhere along the way to the border. A new dam was built in Ethiopia, and a new distribution system was being built to export some of the power from Ethiopia to Kenya to earn foreign exchange and therefore pay off some of the debt required to finance the dam in the first place, but work on the project was halted.

We stopped in Marsabit and found a market and a supermarket, much to our surprise. Just a decade before, this was just a small village, but now that there is a good road to the town, it has improved the facilities in the town. There are more houses, more industry, and more commerce. There is a shopping centre, government offices, distributors of various products, warehouses, and an army barracks. We left town and stopped for lunch overlooking a crater, a former volcano with stunning views.

I wanted to visit Lake Turkana, formerly known as Lake Rudolf. The lake was originally named Lake Rudolf in honour of Crown Prince Rudolf of Austria by Count Sámuel Teleki de Szék and his second-in-command, Lieutenant Ludwig Ritter Von Höhnel, on 6th March 1888. It is a lake in the Kenyan Rift Valley, with its far northern end crossing into Ethiopia. It is the world's largest permanent desert lake and the world's largest alkaline lake. By volume, it is the world's fourth largest salt lake after the Caspian Sea, Issyk-Kul, and Lake Van.

Its continued existence depends on inflows, of the three major rivers that flow into it, including the Omo River, but since the construction of the Gilgel Gibe III Dam in Ethiopia to provide electricity, the lake is likely to shrink. It was just a hundred kilometres to the east, but we would not be visiting it as, despite the better roads that would improve our travel times, there was another problem.

We got to a checkpoint, and the sergeant on duty warned us that there was some tribal conflict in Ethiopia that had spilled over to Kenya, so we ought to check with the police in the next town. We decided to return to Isiolo for the afternoon and camp there overnight to reassess the situation. Meanwhile, we could speak to our minders in Ethiopia and see what the situation really was.

There was a change to the itinerary, but overlanding is always subject to changes in the schedule. After weeks of overlanding, we were used to having our plans altered at the last moment. We found a campsite just out of town called

Henry's Camp, run by a Swiss backpacker who had come here and married a local and had settled down and set up the business. We weren't the only guests that afternoon, as the camp had also been booked for an end of term party by sixth form students from the local school. However, come nightfall, they drifted away, and we had the place to ourselves.

Our local minder and fixer in Ethiopia told us by phone that the trouble was about grazing rights and about who could graze their cattle on some communal land. Sometimes tempers get out of hand, and rival cattle herders shoot each other. There was also an issue where farmers would pick up arms when livestock strayed and ate their crops. It seemed to be a regular occurrence with flare-ups every season for the past nearly thirty years as there is more population growth and limited land resources. The onset of the rainy season eases the pressure on the land as more grazing is available as the rains encourage growth.

One solution, of which I am not sure whether it is wacky, tongue in cheek or scientifically researched, is to improve the electricity supply and the television programmes. Therefore, information is improved, and popular programmes act as a distraction, so people spend less time churning over alleged slights over an open fire, going out and taking action, but staying indoors watching the local equivalent of EastEnders and Coronation Street.

The existing situation is that each village supports their families and neighbours and takes revenge, so with an expanding population putting pressure on land resources, the killing would continue, and the authorities are powerless to create a solution. Trouble flares up for a few weeks until each side has to tend to their cattle, or some other jobs, and incidences reduce, but the bad feeling is still there, so it lingers on until the next confrontation in the next dry season.

We arrived at Moryle, which sits on the border, and there were signs about the new road. The road and the border post had been built by the Chinese. Ethiopia is a landlocked country, and the road we had just come along provides an alternative route to the outside world to Kenya, avoiding ports in Eritrea, Djibouti, and Somalia, which, given some of Ethiopia's history, is a major influence.

Chapter 15
Omo Valley

Our children may learn about the heroes of the past. Our task is to make ourselves the architects of the future.
Jomo Kenyatta

A man who uses force is afraid of reason.
Kenyan proverb

Ethiopia is the most populous landlocked country in the world with a population of 109 million and the second most populous nation on the African continent, ahead of Egypt at 98 million but a long way behind Nigeria, which has a population estimated at 195 million. It traces its roots to the 2nd millennium BC, with a governmental system of monarchy for most of its history.

During the late 19th century Scramble for Africa, Ethiopia was one of only two nations in Africa to retain its sovereignty against long term colonialism by a European colonial power (although it was occupied by Italy between 1936-1941). The other country that escaped colonialism is Liberia, which began as a settlement of the American Colonisation Society, which believed that black people would face better chances for freedom and prosperity in Africa than in the United States. The country declared its independence on 26th July 1847.

King Menelik II became Emperor of Ethiopia in 1889 and ruled until his death in 1913. He made advances in road construction, electricity, education, the development of a central taxation system, and the foundation and building of the city of Addis Ababa, which had become the capital in 1881. After he ascended to the throne in 1889, the city was renamed Addis Ababa, the new capital of Abyssinia.

Menelik had signed the Treaty of Wichale with Italy in May 1889, in which Italy would recognise Ethiopia's sovereignty as long as Italy could control an area north of Ethiopia (modern day Eritrea). In return, Italy was to provide Menelik with weapons and support him as emperor. The Italians used the time between the signing of the treaty and its ratification by the Italian government to expand their territorial claims. This conflict erupted in the Battle of Adwa on 1st March 1896, in which Italy's colonial forces were defeated by the Ethiopians and Italy had to reassess its colonial ambitions.

Ethiopia's independence was interrupted by the Second Italo-Ethiopian War, beginning when it was invaded by Fascist Italy in early October 1935, followed by Italian occupation of the country in 1936. There was some resistance from local guerilla fighting until 1941, when it was liberated by allied forces and Haile Selassie was reinstalled as the absolute monarch of the country.

On 26th August 1942, Haile Selassie issued a proclamation that abolished slavery in Ethiopia. The country had between two and four million slaves in the early 20th century, out of a total population of about eleven million. In 1952, Haile Selassie orchestrated the federation with Eritrea. He dissolved this in 1962 and illegally annexed Eritrea against the UN Federation Agreement. Eritrea fought an armed resistance for three decades and finally won its war of independence in 1993.

In 1974, the Ethiopian monarchy under Haile Selassie was overthrown by the Derg, a Communist military government backed by the Soviet Union led by Mengistu Haile Mariam. The period 1983-85 saw widespread famine, which affected around eight million people and resulted in one million deaths.

Insurrections against Communist rule sprang up, particularly in the northern regions of Eritrea and Tigray. In 1987, the Derg established the People's Democratic Republic of Ethiopia, but it was overthrown in 1991 by the Ethiopian People's Revolutionary Democratic Front, whose forces were advancing on Addis Ababa and Mengistu Haile Mariam, who sought asylum in Zimbabwe, and the Ethiopian People's Revolutionary Democratic Front, which has been the ruling political coalition ever since. In 2006, after a trial that lasted 12 years, Ethiopia's Federal High Court in Addis Ababa found Mengistu guilty of genocide in absentia, and numerous other top leaders of his regime were also found guilty of war crimes.

The Ethiopian calendar, which is approximately seven years and three months behind the Gregorian calendar, co-exists alongside the Borana calendar.

The Borana calendar is a calendrical system once thought to have been used by Borana Oromo, a person living in southern Ethiopia and northern Kenya. The calendar is based upon an earlier Cushitic calendar developed around 300 BC found at Namoratunga. Reconsideration of the Namoratunga site led astronomer and archaeologist Clive Ruggles to conclude that there is no relationship. The Borana calendar consists of 29.5 days and 12 months, for a total of 354 days in a year. The calendar has no weeks but has a name for each day of the month. It is a lunar-stellar calendar system.

While we were at the border, we exchanged money and met our local fixer, Mamo. We had to have a local guide to get us through the trouble area, which we now had to travel through, but the local military would not let us go through the trouble zone without an escort. They didn't want some stray shots causing problems for Mzungus, so we had lunch on the truck whilst we waited for the army to arrange an armed escort. Mzungu was a term that we heard often. It is Bantu for white people. If someone wanted to attract our attention, for instance, in a market, they would shout out 'mzungu' but the expression has no colour bias.

We waited outside the local army base in a truck park with other lorries waiting to go, but without any drivers around. Several trucks full of troops came and went, but eventually one came towards us and turned and beckoned us to follow them. The captain in charge of the truck park came over and told us to follow.

We were escorted out of the border town of Moyale by a military escort from a heavily armed army truck. We were used to driving at around 80 kmph maximum, whereas the military, for strategic reasons, drove at a steady 100 kmph plus and didn't slow down for the speed bumps. Gareth had difficulty keeping up with them, but he persevered. We went through roadblocks with no problems with papers as we had a military escort, and we were therefore just waving through.

Then came the point where they reached the edge of their fiefdom, and they pulled over. We waved goodbye to our escort, and we were once again by ourselves. We drove through more savannah, and it was just like the same scenery that we had seen on the other side of the border. We camped in the gardens of a motel. They were fully booked up, so there were no upgrades available, and on the whole trip, I don't remember anyone asking for an upgrade or being turned away other than here.

As we climbed up into the mountains, part of the road was still being upgraded, so we were diverted along a pleasant country trail, a single track with passing places winding its way up a valley next to a stream. We forded the stream several times until the track reached higher ground and we rejoined the main tarmac road.

This was savannah like scenery, but as we gained altitude, there seemed to be more greenery as it rained more in the mountains. There was evidence of elephants. Not just their football-sized balls of poo, but they had pulled down branches to reach the soft green leaves at the ends of the branches. Several boughs had been bent so far from the trunk that they had snapped off and lay at an angle of 45 degrees from the trunk, and the ends were stripped of all their leaves. Provided that the elephants move on, nature can repair the damage. It is also useful for people roaming through the savannah, as they can use the broken branches for firewood once they have dried.

There were more trees and more lush undergrowth as we continued northwest towards Jinka. The valleys and towering hills were deep as the road snaked its way through the southern highlands. The road was being improved by the Chinese, but it wasn't completed, and huge yellow diggers were moving aggregate about and digging cuttings so that the new road could weave its way along gentle curves. It was very picturesque and one of the best drives that I had experienced for weeks, but its attractions were spoilt by the roadworks and would be spoilt forever once the diggers had finished, and it would just be another motorway driven through some beautiful countryside for traffic to whizz through and ignore.

We arrived at our campsite at the Eyob Hostel and campground in Jinka. We set up the tents, and I got an upgrade as the price was low, but then there wasn't any hot water, the electricity was intermittent, and the free Wi-Fi didn't work. So from that point of view, it wasn't such a great upgrade opportunity.

That evening, our fixer, Mamo, and his driver, Chuchu, took us to a local restaurant to experience injera, spiced vegetables, and a meat dish. Injera is a sourdough risen flatbread with a slightly spongy texture. Traditionally, it is made out of teff flour, a cereal native to Ethiopia, and it is the national dish. It is central to the dining process in local cultures, as bread is the most fundamental component of any meal. I tried it, but if there was a bread option, I would always ask for bread, but as injera is served with every meal, sometimes I just had to eat it or go hungry.

We continued our journey north, heading into the Omo Valley. This little-visited region is home to some of the most colourful ethnic groups in Ethiopia. There are more than a dozen different tribes, each with their own language, traditions, culture, beliefs, and styles of dress, hairstyles and decorative jewellery.

The friendly Hamar people are noted for their ornate, interesting hairstyles, and the Mursi people are famous for their clay lip plates and earlobe decorations. Chuchu drove, and it was advertised to us as a two-hour drive, but in reality, it was three hours. It wasn't far, but the roads were poor—just dirt tracks—and it took us that long to get to our destination.

We were going to visit Mursi village. The tribe's name may not be familiar, but when you mention that they wear lip plates, then everyone knows who you are talking about. We were invited to walk about the village, and Mamo explained some of the customs and would translate for us.

If the children are wearing white clay, then everything is good in that they have food, and their cattle are safe. They are semi-nomadic and grow crops, and go hunting. They always site their villages near a certain tree whose leaves they burn in the evening to ward off mosquitoes. This particular village was sighted in the highlands, and they need to walk tens of kilometres to collect water from the Omo River, but they prefer to live here up in the hills rather than down in the valley, as the temperatures are lower, there are fewer mosquitoes, and there is good agricultural land.

The land is fertile but tires easily, so they need to move on when the land is exhausted. They need to be near their fields to protect both the seeds and the young plants from birds and other animals that would destroy the crop before it could be harvested.

The men sometimes adorn themselves by creating scars, called scarification. But women are so much more active in making themselves more beautiful for their menfolk. They also indulge in scarification, and many of them have interesting strings of scars of geometric designs and patterns on their bodies and occasionally on their arms and legs. They pierce their ears and enlarge the hole to disproportionate extremes by putting in ever larger studs until there are long loops of flesh hanging off.

But the major adornments for women are the lip plates. These are made from clay and decorated using different coloured clays, usually white, red, and black. When a girl is 18 years old, she will have a knife inserted in her skin to separate the lip tissue from the skin coming up from her chin. The community doesn't use any modern medicine, only plants are found in the local environment. Girls that have had the first cut insert a leaf from a particular tree that has healing properties.

In order to determine the passage of time and the number of years, such as for people's age, their unique culture means that they do not have a calendar to determine dates, but ages are measured by how many times the River Omo has flooded in the rainy season, so the chief of the village that I was visiting expressed his age as 38 floodings. I was surprised as he looked a lot older, but then life can be harsh, and it is definitely a tough life for Mursi up in the mountains.

The average life expectancy is about 45 years, that measured against the national average of 65, is poor. They rarely use hospital facilities, preferring to use local medicinal plants. Despite the low life expectancy, death in childbirth is better than the national average, so there is compensation.

Returning to the insertion of the lip plate, the girl's front two bottom teeth are removed using a pointed stick so that the first small lip plate can sit comfortably resting against the remaining two teeth to stretch the loose flap of skin that was the bottom lip. Larger lip plates are added over weeks to stretch the lips and accommodate ever larger lip plates. She can remove the lip plate to eat and sleep, but if she is in public or attends any public event or ceremony, she must wear the lip plate.

An additional ornamentation, that the girls wear is an elaborate headdress. When a man in the community kills a big animal, he becomes a hero of the community. His wife can wear an elaborate headdress that identifies the animal killed. Cape buffalo may be represented by a headdress incorporating the horns of the animal, and a warthog may be shown incorporating the teeth of the animal.

In order to marry a woman, a man has to be able to provide a dowry. This is typically 38 cows and a Kalashnikov. It used to be spears, bows, and arrows but despite the community treasuring their culture, habits, and beliefs, arrows and spears are easy to make and soundless when hunting, but Kalashnikovs are far more effective against large predators and bandits who may be trying to steal their cattle, and their cattle are their most prized possession.

The guns are robust and cheap to manufacture and buy, and ammunition is readily available and cheap. The men in the camp all carried their traditional long sticks, or dingas, used for fighting, but some also had a Kalashnikov hanging over their shoulders. The men wear a blanket hung over their left shoulder, and the women wear a loincloth, but many of the villagers were naked.

Mursi are only allowed one partner. If a wife has been widowed and has not had any children, then she can remarry, but the dowry is only 30 cows. Otherwise, if one of the married couples is deceased, then the surviving partner will remain single. The women would remove their lip plate and cut off the loop of the lip that held it in place.

They grow some plants, such as sorghum and maize, but their wealth and the assessment of a man's worth are determined by the number of cattle that he has. They rarely eat meat, preferring to keep cattle as wealth and drink their milk and blood. There are fish in the river, but they do not eat anything that they cannot see, so they do not eat fish.

The community is fiercely independent. The government wants the children to go to school, but the villagers teach each other all that they need to know to survive in the jungle. They are aware of the internet age, computers, and books but prefer to maintain their culture. They fear that if their children go to school, then their way of life will be radically changed and lost forever.

But I do wonder whether they will be able to survive as they need to move to farm and graze their cattle, but will there be those free open spaces left for them to use as the country becomes ever more developed with new roads, commercial agriculture, mining, urban sprawl, and the constant exposure to tourists with wealth, clothes, cameras, music, and modern amenities that we take for granted such as clean water to drink from a tap, sewage systems, electricity for light and heating, public transport, roofs over our heads, jobs, well stocked supermarkets, and medical care? I support their good intentions, but I fear for their future.

The rot has already started as they accept foreigners into their community. They realise that there are benefits out there for them. There is a charge to visit the village, you can take photos, but it costs you the equivalent of 20 USD cents per person. They need money for bullets, for the Kalashnikovs, for knives, pots, and pans. They need to trade their cattle or any agricultural surplus for the metal bracelets, anklets, and other jewellery that they value and for essential medical care that a suck on a leaf can't cure.

It is a fascinating sight to see and to personally experience, but it won't be there forever, so it may be best to see it now before it is too transformed, along with a lot of other places in the world. Yes, we should visit in as unobtrusive a manner as possible, but we should also become ambassadors to cherish their way of life and not subsume it into the ersatz of modernity where everything is Toyota cars, Coca Cola drinks, Mercedes cars, Suzuki motorbikes, McDonalds burgers, Marlboro cigarettes, and Heineken beer.

Every photo is five Birr, and some of the girls walked around with their hands out, asking for a photo to be taken so that they could get some money. It was easier to just say no. I was also wondering about who would be the subject of my photo, and I felt a bit uncomfortable about taking photos of people—naked children, girls with bare breasts, boys with dicks, topless women—am I am prude? Noah had no qualms and took photos of all the young girls. It was a human zoo, and in retrospect, it was not something that I would ever recommend. I was glad to have had the experience but equally glad to leave.

Chapter 16
En Route to Addis Ababa

The best way to learn to be an independent state is to be an independent state.
Kwarme Nkrumah

A family is like a forest; when you are on the outside, it seems dense but when you are on the inside, you can see that every tree has its place.
Ghanaian proverb

We had a traditional lunch of injera, pickled vegetables, and bean stew. It is a tradition in Ethiopia to be vegan friendly on Wednesdays and Fridays, and restaurants do not serve meat on these days, and butchers are closed.

We were en route to a large market in Keyafer, which is where the Hamar, Tsemay, and Banna tribes have a market. There is a livestock market at the top of the village, which was our first stop. It used to be nearer the centre, but it was too cramped, and it has moved to the outskirts. There were cattle, goats, and sheep for sale. Goats and sheep sell for about USD 100 and cattle for USD 500. When these are transported to Addis Ababa, they can be sold for twice as much.

Some of the animals have distinctive scars in certain patterns and shapes. This is a form of identification, and although the farmers may be illiterate, they can identify their own animals based on their scars. The literacy rate for males is 49% and 29% for females, and although low in international terms, this is an improvement over the last decade.

Then we walked down the main road and went to the open-air market. Here there are clothes stalls, honey sellers, fruit and vegetables sellers, cafes selling local beer made from maize and a drink made from honey. The cafes are popular places for the farmers when they have finished their business in the livestock market further up the road. There are coffee shops and souvenir sellers. You can get most of what you might want from the market.

The Tsemay tribe women typically wear a large belt of cowrie shells around their neck and a shaped leather skirt. The unmarried girls wear clothes made from cotton or leather. The men wear a sarong type garment with strings of beads around their necks and arms. Mamo stopped one lady at random in traditional dress and negotiated a price, and then she posed for us to take photos.

We had enough time to have some of the honey drink and a locally brewed coffee in the market before we headed out of town. We stopped at the roadside for a natural break, and it looked deserted, but in no time at all, there were more than half a dozen locals staring at us. Remember that TIA and there is always a local not far away who will be inquisitive enough to come and watch the Mzungus.

We continued on to Turmi, where there is a market for the Hamer tribe. We arrived too late to see much of any interest, as the market had finished, and the stall holders were packing up. Then we went a little way up the road to stay in a Hamer village. They were waiting for us just outside the village, and a number of children shouted, waved, and followed us as we made our way into the village. They were all as interested in us as we were in them.

They raise cattle and goats but also plant maize, sorghum, beans, and pumpkins. The children herd the animals, and the women are responsible for collecting water, cooking, and looking after the household and the children. The men look after the herds, do the ploughing, and tend to the hives. The hives are cylindrical wicker baskets often placed in acacia trees as they are strong enough to support the hives, which can weigh up to 50 kilogrammes each with the amount of honey that the bees can collect.

I was interested in the mechanics of these wicker baskets, as bees have been kept for centuries, but in Europe, straw skeps were used to create a pointed dome. The problem was that to get to the honey, the beekeeper would have to break the skep apart and rehouse the bees in a new skep, where they would have to fashion a new honeycomb hanging from the top of the skep in which to store their honey.

Despite centuries of beekeeping, the modern beehive, with its removable and reusable supers above the brood box and the frames inside that we all recognise today, was only invented in 1851 by Reverend Lorenzo Langstroth, a priest from Massachusetts. Each frame inside the super could also be pre-made with the base of the honeycomb, saving the bee's time and effort, and all they had to do was build up the honeycomb from the base layer and store their honey inside.

The women wear goatskin, which is elaborately decorated with beads and cowrie shells. They also wear strings of beads around their necks, waists, and bracelets, typically a mixture of black and red beads (as opposed to the Banna, who typically have black and blue beads). The married women wear necklaces around their necks. Men are allowed several wives, and all married women wear two solid metal necklaces, but the first wife also wears a leather bound torque above the two solid necklaces to signify her status.

All of the Hamar people have distinctive hair styles. The hair is turned into small, tight, and short dreadlocks and pasted with red ochre clay. They paint their bodies with white clay to make interesting shapes, usually associated with ceremonial events. The men can be seen carrying a small mushroom-like wooden object that doubles as a stool during the day and a pillow at night.

We walked around the village with a guide who told us about their lifestyle and how they lived. The goats were herded into enclosures with thick walls of acacia thorns overnight. The cattle and donkeys are less venerable to predators, so they stay the night behind a raised earthwork about waist height with a scattering of acacia thorns on the outside face.

We saw the cemetery at the top of a hill overlooking the village and the surrounding countryside. We looked inside several of the huts. Unlike Mursi, who had tiny huts for the family, these were spacious and had an upper story for storage. The Mursi huts were low and made of reed on a wooden frame. Hamer huts have lengths of branches driven into the ground to act as walls with gaps between the branches, reaching up as high as your waist to chest height, and then a circular domed roof on top of the structure made from reed.

We tried some of the coffee that they produce. One of the senior men's second wives run a coffee shop from her hut. She had a small fire and a boiling pot on the open fire. We crawled in through the small entrance and sat on hides, but there was not enough room to stand upright, so we had to be careful not to bang our heads.

The coffee was scooped out of the large pot by a ladle and served in a gourd or half a pumpkin that had been hollowed out and dried in the sun. These don't sit neatly on the floor, but her answer to that was to thread beer bottle tops onto a wire and bend them into a circle, and the curved surface of the pumpkin sits in the central hollow of the circular ring of beer bottle tops. They don't use the coffee beans but just the husks, which are boiled in water and served without sugar or milk. The coffee beans are valuable and are sold at the local market.

We put our tents up in the village, watched by half of the village, with the kids wanting to help but having no idea how to put up a tent. Eventually our guide shooed the kids away, and we were left to cook supper, but they still watched from a distance, just outside the pool of light cast by the lights above the cooking area, as if it were a live show in a theatre or a cinema.

We were to have another village tour early in the morning, at dawn. The donkeys and cattle are released early, but the goats are not taken to pasture until they have been milked. We passed a few enclosures where all the family was busy milking, with the exception of the smallest children, who played in the dirt or walked through the herd in the enclosure to pick out the next animal to be milked.

The milker places the hind leg of a goat behind their knee and squats. Thus, the animal is immobile, and the milker has uninterrupted access to the teats and milks the goat into a bucket, which is used raw for breakfast. Then we set off for what turned out to be a long walk for nearly an hour to the local river.

The river was dry, but if you dig in the sandy riverbed, water will flow into the bottom of the hole. It is initially dirty, but if you scoop out the first drop of water to fill it, the water becomes cool and clear and can be drunk straight away without treatment. By this time, the morning was heating up, and it was another long walk back to the village. We were much later for breakfast than intended, and we had to grab a slice of bread and a banana to eat on the truck and pack the tent away so as not to be late for the morning departure.

We were going back largely the way we had come to rejoin the main road from Kenya to the capital, Addis Ababa. Parts were tarmac, and we had a good time, but some sections were just gravel, so we had to go slowly for comfort. We stopped for the night in Arba Minch, which translates as 'Forty Springs'. It is located on the western side of the Great Rift Valley, at an elevation of 1,285 metres above sea level. It sits between two large lakes in Ethiopia, Chamo Lake and Abaya Lake, which will be the country's fourth largest lake.

It used to be the third largest lake until the Grand Ethiopian Renaissance Dam on the Blue Nile was built starting in 2011, and the dam will be the largest hydroelectric power plant in Africa when completed, as well as the 7th largest in the world. As of August 2017, the work stood at 60% completion, but once completed, the reservoir will take 5 to 15 years to fill with water and will reduce Abaya Lake's ranking to fourth.

Opposite the city on the isthmus between the two lakes is the Nechisar National Park. It is home to zebras, Grant's gazelle, dik-dik, and the greater kudu, as well as one of the last three populations of the endangered Swayne's hartebeest, endemic to Ethiopia. There are also bushbucks, bushpigs, Anubis baboons, velvet monkeys, and black-backed jackals. A stretch of the northwest shore of Lake Chamo is known as the Crocodile Market, where hundreds of crocodiles gather to bask. It has populations of kingfishers, storks, pelicans, flamingos, and African fish eagles, and the area is an important habitat for migrating birds.

Arba Minch is known as an area of fruit farms, including mango, banana, orange, apple, guava, and pineapple. Its other main agricultural produce, for which it is well known, is its fish farms, which contribute to the country's more than 15,000 tons of freshwater fish produced annually.

It was a cold night, but we had put our flysheets on, so once you got into the tent and used body heat to warm up the inside, it was quite pleasant. I was always surprised that this was summer in Africa, yet it was cold. It was warmer in the UK than here in Ethiopia, but it was the rainy season, and we were at altitude. Over the next two days, cook groups left early, straight after breakfast, to go shopping. The rest of us had a leisurely breakfast and packed everything away, and then we drove into the centre of town to pick up the cook groups and their purchases.

We set off along the main road towards Addis Ababa. The main road is a dull, purpose-built highway with little to see, so we diverted off the new main road onto the old road through Soho and Hosana, which took us through several towns and past fields of maize, bananas, and sorghum. There is rain here, and the soils are fertile and productive, so even on the steeper slopes there are terraces, and every bit of land seems to be in cultivation.

The road picks its way around hills and up steep slopes, so sometimes we had wonderful views across valleys but were going at a snail's pace as the truck ground its way up the steep slopes. Going down wasn't any better, as Gareth had to keep in a low position to maintain control, although the other lorry drivers overtook us at breakneck speeds and on corners without being able to see whether any traffic was coming.

We turned off the road to have a picnic lunch in a forest, and although there was no one to see and no buildings nearby, TIA and I was soon surrounded by two dozen inquisitive locals, mainly women and children but some teenagers and men. They were not threatening but just curious, with the occasional smile and wave and a lot of talking amongst themselves. It can be intimidating for newbies to be surrounded by a lot of black people dressed in rags holding machetes, but we were used to this by now, and we were polite, engaging in some small talk. We moved on through Hosana and to Worabe. This is a densely populated area, and we couldn't find a bush camp, so we asked to camp in the grounds of a hotel.

There wasn't enough space for all of us, so we all upgraded to rooms. There was in fact enough space using some spare land around the back of the hotel, but not for all of us, and the manager didn't want us parking some of our tents on his nicely manicured lawns and next to his flowerbeds at the front of the hotel.

It was an odd place as it had a range of single storey rooms around one courtyard with parking in the middle, tea available from a stall with a rundown air about it with peeling paint, a kiddie's playground with the rides in need of repair, and several open fronted marquees with groups of men chewing quat. Then in the next compound was a three storey modern concrete-built block of rooms with ensuite facilities and beautiful gardens.

The rooms weren't that great. I needed to recharge my laptop, my camera batteries, and my head torch, but only one of the three sockets in the room worked. Two of the four light bulbs in the room didn't work. There was no hot water. The toilet had a cistern, but it didn't work, but luckily there was a large bucket of water and a plastic jug to use to flush the toilet. Except there was no way to refill the bucket other than to put it under the shower. It worked in fashion, but the water from the shower head went in every direction, and only a little actually fell in the bucket, but lots of it splashed onto the floor as there was no shower curtain, TIA. But at least I had a restful night in bed until the muezzin called the faithful to prayer in the morning, an hour before sunrise.

Back on the road to the capital, Addis Ababa, we passed through Bitutiya, and outside of the town, we stopped at Tiya. It is a UNESCO designated site and home to several stelae. These are the graves of several high-class burials. Each of the stones are raised above the grave of an important individual. There is a common standard for interpreting the stone carvings. The carvings on the stone include swords, circles, a symbol similar to a Greek letter, and a symbol similar to a banana tree.

The swords indicate how many of the enemies the individual killed. The circles are the nipples of the warriors, indicating that the incumbent of the grave is a male. The Greek letter is a representation of his ribs, and the palm-like symbol is either the false palm that grows locally or the pillow that we have seen many members of the Hamer tribe carry with them wherever they go. The ancient tribes left no written records, so much of the interpretation is only interpretation and is subject to intellectual debate.

Our second stop of the day was at the Adadi Mariam rock-hewn church. The town that hosts this church also hosts a weekly market, which unfortunately was the day that we turned up to see the church. This is the only church that was cut from the rock by King Lalibela outside of the clutch of churches that were hewn from the rock in the town that still uses his name.

The site was selected due to the rock that was available. Unlike the churches in Lalibela, which are cut from basalt, the rock here is sandstone. This site was constructed after the other churches in Lalibela and was the last one to be built by King Lalibela. The outside of the church was started and cut into the sandstone in the 11th century. The block left standing was then hollowed out to form a walkway with arches looking out into the ditch that surrounded the site. Then a general assembly area was created within the 'block'. An area was carved from the block to serve as an area where communion was taken, and there was another door into the inner sanctum that was not open to worshippers and is not open to the public.

We had lunch on the grounds of the church and then packed everything away. We would be in a hotel in Addis Ababa for several days, so we would not be doing any cooking, so we donated all our leftover fresh fruit and vegetables to the church. Then we left Adadi Mariam and drove for another two hours into Addis Ababa. There were wide roads, but there was also a lot of traffic, but we made it to our hotel in the old section of the city.

Addis Ababa means a new flower or natural spring, depending on the language that you claim the name comes from. I prefer new flowers, as the site was not ideal due to the lack of firewood and the absence of springs for fresh water. The city is host to the headquarters of the African Union, the new organisation that grew out of the Organisation of African Unity (OAU), and the headquarters of the United Nations Economic Commission for Africa (ECA), as well as various other continental and international organisations. The site of

Addis Ababa was chosen by Empress Taytu Betul, and the city was founded in 1886 by Emperor Menelik II.

That evening, it was the football World Cup Final, and a large section of the group went off to watch the match in a local bar. We had shared rooms in the hotel for the next few nights, but I had upgraded to a suite in the Taitu Hotel, the oldest hotel in the capital, having been built in 1898. It was a fascinating piece of architecture, and the rooms were all rustic. I had half thought about taking a room in a local international four-star hotel such as Heather and David had opted for, but after I inspected the rooms on offer at the Taitu Hotel, I opted to stay in the quirky and authentic original hotel despite the rather poor facilities and the unknown factor of whether the shower actually worked and whether the hot tap in the shower was just for show.

We had been allocated basic rooms with a shared bathroom, adequate but no hot water, and draughty in one of the annexes to the main building. In contrast, the main building was built in 1898 as a hotel, and it had faded charm and was architecturally interesting. I was prepared to pay for an upgrade in a nearby modern hotel, but seeing the original building with its elegant charm, although in need of refurbishment, I opted for an upgrade to a room with ensuite facilities in the original part of the hotel. I looked at several of the available rooms and specified which one I wanted. It was on the corner of the building, furthest away from the stairs, with a balcony. Being the corner room, the balcony went around the corner of the building, and I had a dual aspect balcony.

Since I had upgraded and I discovered that I had hot water, and I knew that the basic rooms only had communal showers with cold water, I was only too happy to let Zac and Noodles and anybody else use my bathroom facilities.

I went with Kim to the Sudanese embassy. We weren't sure whether we would all be required to attend in person, so the rest of the group hung around the hotel, dressed in their best, ready for an embassy visit if required. Once Kim and I discovered that people weren't required in person, she texted the group that it was a free day for them, and she handed in all the passports, visa request forms, and money to the embassy official, and then we got a taxi back to the hotel. I got out on the way back to explore 'El Mercato', one of East Africa's largest open-air markets.

I had been to the Kumasi market in Ghana, which claims to be the largest market in Africa, and Karatina, in Kenya, which claims to be the largest market in Africa, and then there is another claim that the largest market is El Mercato in

Addis Ababa. There are so many claims that one particular market is the biggest. I was inspired to check, but without an authoritative source to confirm my research, I am still at a loss as to which is actually the largest open-air market in Africa.

Somehow, I had lost my hotel room key. I would have to pay for a replacement, so I waited before showing up at reception. I had taken my clothes to the local laundry, which was surprisingly very expensive, and the price doubled when I said that I wanted them back the same day. I had given them everything to wash and only had the clothes I stood up in. I hoped that my hotel key was in one of the pockets of my laundry. It turned out to be a cold and wet day. I was surprised that despite being not far from the equator and July, which was summer in the northern hemisphere, it was cold, and I needed a fleece. Admittedly, Addis Ababa is at an elevation of 2,350 metres, but it was still cold.

I had to waste a day without access to my hotel room and hang around cafes and bars. I collected my washing, and searched my pockets, and sure enough, I found the hotel room key in a pocket. On reflection, the cost of a new key was just a few dollars, and I could have just paid it, got back into my room to collect my camera and guide book, and gone sightseeing, so I had wasted a day, but I had a chance of an enforced 'chill day' and you need one every so often.

It rained for most of the night and only got better mid-morning when the rain eased off and finally stopped. The bad weather blew over, and it became a bright, sunny day. I went for a guided walking tour of the city on my last full day in Addis Ababa.

Our planned departure was scheduled as an early start with breakfast in the dark next to the truck. It was still raining, so we had to move breakfast from next to the truck, which was in the open, into a sheltered area of the hotel. The whole group was back together. Heather and David had signed out of their five-star hotel to slum it with our overlanders. Noah had completed his side tour to the Afar Depression, and Mike had returned from his diving expedition in the Red Sea.

We once again had a full complement, and as it was still raining, Gareth set off to drive out of Addis Ababa, but those of us sitting in the back of the truck were disadvantaged as it was cold, and with the sides down to try to keep some heat in and the rain out, we couldn't see much through the plastic windows with rain running down the outside.

We drove out of the city and into the hills, and somewhere along the road in the morning the rain stopped, and we buzzed Gareth to stop so that we could roll up the sides. It was still cold, and we sat wearing fleeces, coats, and sleeping bags to keep warm, but at least we could now see some of the scenery. It was a very scenic drive through some dramatic scenery, with rolling hills and deep valleys as we made our way northwest from Addis Ababa towards Bahir Dar, which would be a two-day drive.

The plateau is about 2,500 metres high, with rolling grazing land and very few trees. Someone buzzed for a stop for a pee, but in an area like this with no cover, finding a convenient stopping place with some privacy was going to be difficult. The rule was to buzz, but not at the last minute, as it was often then case a convenient pee stop might not be available for another twenty minutes.

Gareth would pull over and stop when he found a suitable place. Up here in the open wilderness, there were few suitable places, but Gareth stopped in a cutting that might give the girls some privacy. Such is gender inequality that it seems that men can pee anywhere, but girls require some cover. The girls had their first choice and opted to go down the embankment leading up to the cutting to be out of sight of oncoming traffic, and the boys were left to widdle into the ditch at the side of the road in sight of all passing traffic.

We reached the gorge of the Blue Nile, which has cut a deep gorge through the mountains. The bottom of the valley is at an elevation of 1,200 metres, so it is a drop of 1,300 metres from the plateau to the river. The road reaches the edge of the rift and plummets down the steep sided gorge. It had been raining, and there was still a lot of cloud about. The only views we got were brief glimpses when the clouds parted for a while. We inched our way down the side of the gorge in bottom gear for kilometres after kilometres.

We finally saw the Blue Nile, which was a churning mass of muddy brown water with nothing blue about it. It had been raining for several days, and the river was swollen with the runoff from the rains in the mountains. There are two bridges here across the river. The original bridge was built by the Italians and still stands, but it is not used. There is a newer bridge literally just upstream, built by the Japanese, a cable stayed bridge across the gulf. The road crosses the river and then follows a tributary valley back up to the plateau.

We inched up the steep inclines in bottom gear and were once again on the plateau. The scenery changed again with a large area of flat agricultural land, and it seemed that every inch was under the plough. There was water between the freshly ploughed furrows. There was mist rising from the fields due to the difference in temperature between the air and the waterlogged fields. The ditches and streams were swollen with muddy water as it rushed off the plateau, a testament to the recent heavy rains. The road from Addis Ababa northwards would have been a very scenic route, but much of it was bathed in cloud and rain.

We passed through the large market town of Debre Markos, and then we started looking for a bush camp. This was always going to be difficult as the area is a fertile farming area and the population density is quite high, so trying to find somewhere out of the way would be a challenge.

We found an old road that we would have to take. It didn't tick all the boxes, but it was the best it was in the circumstances. The road crossed a steep valley diagonally. But the slope was so steep that the ground had slipped in several places. The verge had disappeared, and the foundations and the tarmac were slowly crumbling into the void below. The municipality's road builders had dug into the hillside higher up the slope and had built another loop of road ten to twenty metres into the hill, leaving the old loop of road redundant but also partially hidden from the new road. The verge on the uphill side of the road had been left, and it was flat and wide enough for our tents.

We set up the awning and started cooking just as some local farmers were herding their cattle along the old road and through our campsite to get back home. We smiled and waved, and they stopped for a while to chat and exchange stories before herding their cattle back into a close-knit herd and back to their evening quarters.

Chapter 17
Simien Mountains

We are here to do good to others. What the others are here for, I have no idea.
W H Auden

If we stand tall, it is because we stand on the backs of those who came before us.

Often quoted by Nelson Mandela, this is a widespread and old African proverb

It was another cold and wet morning as we drove on to Bahir Dar. I was wearing two fleeces because it was so cold. I have mentioned this before, but it was still incredible to me that this was summer in the northern hemisphere, and we were about halfway between the Tropic of Cancer and the Equator, but it was cold and wet, and Bahir Dar is at an elevation of circa 1,800 metres.

We had arrived in Bahir Dar, which is located on the southern edge of Lake Tana, which, after Lake Turkana, is the second-largest lake in Ethiopia and is the source of the Blue Nile. The lake is up to 84 kilometres long and 66 kilometres wide and covers 3.200 square kilometres. Its surface is at an elevation of 1,788 metres, and the lake is up to 15 metres deep. There are boat trips to some of the small islands, which have monasteries dating back up to 900 years, and which are still looked after by monks who live from subsistence farming. Another boat trip on offer could take visitors to see the Blue Nile Falls.

Our scheduled camping option was not available due to the redevelopment of the hotel, and the new management claimed to know nothing of our booking and declined to allow us to camp on what was left of their grounds. We moved on to Dib Anbessa, a purpose-built older hotel near the city centre. We parked in the courtyard and set up the awning. We were allowed to cook that evening by the hotel management as we had already bought the food, but our other meals would be a buy your own option in the hotel.

It was charming inside. The outside was of a modern design and built with concrete. Inside, there was a lot of wood panelling in both the bar and the restaurant, with deep, heavily stuffed chairs, so it had the air of a Victorian Club.

Our guide collected six of us—Mat, Sarah, both Deb, Jacci, and me—and we walked down to a waiting boat on the shoreline. It was a slow boat, and several other boats overtook us. We were going to see some monasteries that were set around the lake, some on peninsulas and some on islands.

It took more than an hour and a half to get to the first site, which was the Betremariam Monastery on a peninsular. We walked from the dock up to visit a small museum before moving on to the monastery itself. It had a walled compound, and inside was a round thatched building made from timber with walls infilled with mud on the wattle. Inside was a square building with twelve doors into the inner sanctuary. There were brightly coloured paintings of scenes from the Bible, with lots of red, blues, and yellows. The building is over 800 years old, but the paintings are just 300 years old.

A short distance away is the Entos Eyesu Monastery on a small island. This one was stone-built and had a circular, single-storey structure. Inside, one half of the building was where the congregation stood, and the other half had a walled inner sanctum with a passageway all around it. There was another museum and some ancillary buildings.

We were about to motor to another monastery, but by popular consent, we had seen enough ecclesiastical buildings, so we opted to skip it. Instead, we motored to the outflow from the lake, which is the source of the Blue Nile. We motored some distance down the Nile. There were some hippopotamus in the water, which we steered well clear of and gave them a wide berth before turning around and heading back to the docks. I stopped at a few shops on the way back to the hotel. I needed a new pair of flip flops. I had slipped in some mud at one of the monasteries and had broken the thong between the toes.

We drove along one side of the lake and then through the mountains to Lalibela. This was one of the most breathtaking scenic routes in Ethiopia and even better than reaching Bahir Dar with its forests, steep mountains, and deep valleys. It was absolutely stunning, but the occasional low cloud obscured some of the mountain tops.

En route to the town, there was a lot of construction and road work. The road was being widened and straightened, and therefore it went through some people's farms, houses, and small holdings. The people affected had been paid compensation, so they had money to rebuild or add extensions, so there were lots of partially completed buildings.

We arrived at our campsite in the centre of Lalibela in the afternoon, the Tukul Village Hostel. We weren't going to visit the churches until the next day to give us enough time to see them all. After breakfast the next morning, we walked up the road, produced our passports for identification, paid our entrance fee, and a guide escorted us around the site and informed us about the various churches.

Lalibela is famous for its 11 monolithic rock-hewn churches and is one of Ethiopia's holiest cities. Ethiopia was one of the earliest nations to adopt Christianity in the first half of the fourth century, although the churches date from the seventh to the thirteenth centuries. King Lalibela built several of the churches, and they are all different designs. One of the churches has a modern free-standing roof built over the original church to keep the rain off. Another church is carved into the rock but has a stone-built façade, whilst the Church of St George, a cruciform church, is unique and the best known of all the churches. It was a long tour lasting all morning, but we came away awestruck by the amount of work that had been required to chisel these great pieces of architecture from the living rock.

We had seen ten of the eleven original rock-hewn churches by lunchtime (the last church is some distance out of town), so we walked up to the Lookout Restaurant, perched on the end of a ridge with views up and down the valley. It has an unusual architectural design, with sloping, curved walkways to connect the different levels. There was some seating outside, but we opted for some inside tables as there were clouds and the weather forecast suggested that it was due to rain from lunchtime onwards.

As it happened, the rain held off until the evening, and it rained continually overnight with some thunder and lightning, and we had to take down our tents in the rain and pack them away wet. We drove back the way we had come and were treated to another spectacular drive through mountains, across a large plateau, and more spectacular mountains before reaching more gentle ground to the north of Lake Tana enroute for Gondar, which was the capital of Ethiopia from 1632 until 1868.

We spent a night in a community-based hostel, part of the Awra Amba community founded by Zumra Nuru in 1980, with 19 other followers who shared his vision. They aim to get out of poverty by education and hard work and promote gender equality and non-religious tolerance. In fact, their village income is twice that of neighbouring traditional villages. Now more than 520 live in the community. Everything is owned by the community, such as the houses and land on which the village sits. There is some industry, such as a weaving factory, a mill, a guest house, and farming. It is not for everyone, so people can join, but they can also leave if it is not for them.

There was a heavy downpour, and the sound of rain hitting the metal roof echoed inside the guest house in which we were staying, and we were all awake well before breakfast. We had hot water for drinks from kettles boiled on gas, as the wood was damp, but we used some charcoal in a small pot boiler to get enough hot water for the whole group. After breakfast, we had a brief presentation on the community from its founder and a tour of the weaving factory and the souvenir shop.

Then it was another drive through the mountains to Gondar, where we arrived in the afternoon to find our hotel, named the L Shaped Hotel. We crossed the road to a travel agent, and we squeezed into his small office. He ordered tea from the cafe next door and explained the details of the trip to the Simien Mountains National Park. Not everyone wanted to go or had the budget to pay for it, but I wanted to go, so I booked the trip into the mountains to leave the next morning.

That evening, we all went to a local upmarket restaurant just a short walk up the road for a traditional meal. It was served buffet style, and there was a large range of dishes, regrettably without the local name of the dish, whether it was meat, fish, or salad. There was also a dance display, accompanied by some local musicians, traditional instruments, and music for entertainment. There were many other guests, so it was a popular place and must have been featured in several guidebooks.

Gareth had some work to do on the truck, but those of us who had booked the mountain trek got into a minivan and were driven for a scenic two-hour journey through rolling agricultural land towards the Simien Mountains National Park.

The park was created in 1969 and covers 220 square kilometres and includes Ras Dashan, which, at 4,550 metres, is the highest point in Ethiopia. It is home to a number of endangered species, including the Ethiopian wolf and the Walia ibex, a wild goat found nowhere else in the world.

We stopped in Debark at the National Park offices to collect our tickets, permits, and two armed guards. We were introduced to our driver, Kuncho, and our guide, who was called Vosi, who both spoke English, but we were not introduced to our two armed guards, and I learnt that whilst they were with us to ensure our safety, they didn't speak any English and they spoke a local language that I had never come across.

We left the town and started to climb up into the hills on a dirt road and turned off to enter the Simien Mountains National Park through an arch with an armed guard who checked our passports, permits, and tickets very carefully against his daily schedule of visitors, guides, and guards, ticking each one off before letting us through. Whilst he seemed alone, I noticed that there was a bevy of other heavily armed soldiers sheltering from the rain under an awning behind the main building.

We stopped at the edge of a steep cliff with vertical drops of between 500 metres and 1,500 metres. These mountains are home to Gelada monkeys, originally called baboons but now known as monkeys, after eight years of a ten-year research project by Minnesota University.

We hadn't walked for five minutes from the car park when we saw our first troop of monkeys. They eat grass, which makes up 95% of their diet. They aren't tame, but they are quite tolerant of humans. They spent a lot of their time foraging, although there were occasional scuffles as the troupe worked their way through the grass and in between the occasional tree and bush. It was quite atmospheric, as there were thick clouds and fog all afternoon.

We had a long walk along the edge of the cliff and saw more monkeys. We eventually reached our campsite, which was a series of huts on top of the cliff. Around late afternoon, the cloud cleared, and we had great views down the valley. This is typical weather for this area in the rainy season. It is clear in the morning, but clouds bubble up in the late morning. It then rains, and afterwards the clouds clear for dusk. Although the weather is fickle, it doesn't always follow this pattern.

We settled down in the evening, and whilst we sat inside with a feeble fire that struggled to change the temperature inside the cabin, our two armed guards sat outside to protect us for most of the evening. We had speculated why they were there, whether to stop us from picking flowers, to protect us from predators such as leopards and bands of hyenas or bandits, or whether it was just to produce jobs. We sat around and chatted until late into the night when they came into the hut and bedded down next to the door, and that was our cue to go to bed.

It was cold in the poorly insulated hut and at this altitude. It was also noisy, as there were quite a few snorers. I was up early, and as there was no running water, I shaved in cold water, using as little as possible from my drinking bottle and with the help of a small handheld mirror. I shaved every day, but all the other men just grew a beard whilst we travelled through Africa.

We set out from camp along the edge of the cliff to a waterfall. The weather started out cold and damp, but the fog cleared after a couple of hours, and then we had spectacular views from the cliffs and very scenic vistas along the face of the cliffs. We walked up the road, were collected by our driver at the top, and were driven to the next camp site. This was a more substantial affair, with several rooms off a central communal area. There were some other guests there when we arrived, but they would be leaving in the morning. There was a Dutch couple, Boah and Dirk, and a German girl called Maria. They each had a room to themselves, but there weren't enough rooms and beds, so they had to share with some of us.

I went for a short walk, but it started to rain, so I turned back and got back just before the rain turned into a monsoon. Some of the others who had gone for a walk were not so lucky and got thoroughly soaked. There was no heating in the hut, so wet things were hung up, but with just body heat, it would make little difference, so the clothes would still be wet in the morning.

The beds in this hut were a lot closer together than the hut on the first night and squeezed into the small rooms, but it was still cold and there were too many snorers. From our base camp at 3,600 metres, we walked up Mount Bwahit, whose summit is 4,437 metres, which makes it the park's second highest mountain. There were low clouds and fog, and we saw very little, but it was clearing slowly. There is a wide track that runs up towards the summit for vehicles, although the track turns before the summit to cross a high-level pass. It took a few curves to make a steady gradient, but we would take the short cut straight up the slope, which was steeper but not so far to walk. We were looking for animals but didn't see any.

We left the track to follow a footpath across boulders that led to the summit. Soon, we were scrambling across boulders to reach the top. By the time we reached the top, the cloud had cleared, and we could see right across the park and in the distance Ethiopia's highest peak, Ras Dashan. But to reach the top of that mountain, you need the right equipment and to be experienced mountaineers.

Our trip back to Gondar was not as quick as it had been to get to the Simien Mountains National Park. There were reports of violence and demonstrations. The director in charge of the new dam construction on the Nile, Simegnew Bekele, had threatened to invite journalists to the site and expose some of the corruption and backhanders that had been made, and he had been assassinated in Addis Ababa. He was a popular figure and had come from Gondar. Some of the roads were closed by police or blocked by demonstrations.

We waited in Debark to check on the security situation in Gondar. It was a bad sign, but there was no traffic on the road coming from Gondar. It was felt that the demonstrations would be over by the time we got there, so after waiting a while, we set off. There was still no traffic coming in the opposite direction, but as we approached the outskirts, the road was covered in rocks and branches, and a tree trunk had been left blocking one side of the road, causing traffic to take it in turns to pass the obstruction. There was plenty of evidence of a demonstration, but nobody was about. Everywhere was eerily quiet, the pavement was empty, and there was no traffic coming towards us. It was quite a contrast to the bustle when we first arrived.

The political situation was also in a state of flux as there had been new developments within the government, which was more tolerant of political differences. Eritrea had fought an independence war for three decades against Ethiopia and a two-year long, border war, and there was a lot of animosity between the two countries. However, whilst we were there, Ethiopia, headed by Prime Minister Abiy Ahmed, agreed to fully implement the peace treaty signed with Eritrea in 2000 that would define the border between the two countries and, significantly, had agreed to establish diplomatic links.

We reached our hotel, and the staff said that the streets were too dangerous and that we should not go out. But that was easier said than done, as there were only snacks at the bar, and we had not been food shopping. Therefore, we went out in one large group for security and went back to the same restaurant that we had visited when we had first arrived in Gondar. It was the same buffet style offering of local dishes, but this time without the floor show of musicians and dancers, and we were the only diners there all evening.

Chapter 18
Across the Sahara

I have always thought that underpopulated countries in Africa are vastly polluted.
Lawrence Summers

When the crocodile smiles, be extra careful.
African proverb

We left the L Shaped Hotel and drove through mountains to get to the border with Sudan. We had a truck lunch to use the last of the fresh fruit and vegetables. We also had a sweep of the truck to ensure that there was no wine or beer inadvertently left on board. Sudan is Muslim and legally dry, and alcohol is illegal with dire sanctions if you are found with alcohol, so we made doubly sure there was none left on the truck. Then we drove on and presented ourselves at the border. We had the usual range of forms to complete and biometrics to be taken, and then we went into Sudan.

It was nothing like what I had expected. The area of Sudan is a flat, fertile agricultural country with black soil and sufficient rainfall to grow a range of crops. After the rain, cold, and altitudes of Ethiopia, Sudan is much lower in altitude, and it was noticeably warmer, perhaps fifteen to twenty degrees warmer.

We bush camped in a former quarry where they had dug out the rock to use as aggregate for the road. The road was old, potholed, and in need of maintenance. The ground had a thin covering of gravel over a solid rock floor, and it was hard to drive the tent pegs in. There was a strong breeze through the gap between the fly and the tent itself, although it was beneficial as it had a cooling effect.

That evening, most of the group went to bed after the evening meal. There was no beer or wine to tempt the night owls to stay up. I stayed up with Noodles, but we felt that we were disturbing everyone else as we were talking, and they had gone to bed, so we went to bed early as well.

We had passed through Al Qadarif and Wad Madani, and the closer we got to Khartoum, the better the road became. This is the capital of Sudan and is a major urban centre for more than five million people out of a country population of 37 million. It is located at the confluence of the White Nile, flowing north from Lake Victoria, and the Blue Nile, flowing west from Ethiopia. The origin of the city name is in dispute, depending on which language you want to claim was the original one to name the city. My favourite is the local Dinka word "Khar-tuom" which translates as "place where rivers meet" which given that two major rivers met here in an arid landscape, and it is the major feature that might inspire naming the location.

The city was founded in 1821, when Khartoum was established 24 kilometres north of the ancient city of Soba, by Ibrahim Pasha, the son of Egypt's ruler, Muhammad Ali Pasha, who had just incorporated Sudan into his realm. Originally, Khartoum served as an outpost for the Egyptian Army, but the settlement quickly grew into a regional centre of trade, and it became a focal point for the local slave trade.

On 13th March 1884, troops loyal to the Mahdi, Muhammad Ahmad, started a siege of Khartoum, against defenders led by British General Charles George Gordon. The siege lasted ten months until 26th January 1885, when the Mahdists broke into the city and massacred the Anglo-Egyptian garrison. The city was subsequently retaken by Lord Kitchener, and order was restored.

Sudan gained independence in 1953 after it was ruled by a series of unstable parliamentary governments and military regimes. Under Gaafar Nimeiry, Sudan instituted Islamic law in 1983. This exacerbated the rift between the Arab north, the seat of government, and the black African animists and Christians in the south. Differences in language, religion, ethnicity, and political power erupted into civil war between government forces and the Sudan People's Liberation Army (SPLA), eventually concluding in the independence of South Sudan in 2011. Sudan used to be the largest country in Africa, but after the independence of South Sudan, it is now only the third largest country on the continent after Algeria and Mauritania.

Our camp in the city was on the banks of the Nile at the quirky but interesting Blue Nile Sailing Club. It houses one of General Kitchener's old gunboats, a relic from the British military campaign against the Mahdi over a century ago that he used in the battle of Omdurman in 1898. It has been hauled up onto the bank overlooking the Blue Nile. The bow gun can still be seen, but it is not open to the public, and the more than one hundred years since her epic battle have seen her decay, and she is in need of some restoration and refurbishment.

Our evening meal was arranged by our local minder and fixer, Midhat, at a local restaurant. There was a long delay waiting to get taxis and another long delay getting served despite pre-ordering the food, but then TIA. We had kisra, a popular thin fermented bread made from durra, or wheat. There are two different forms of kisra, either thin baked sheets, known as kisra rhaheeefa, which is similar to injera, or porridge known as kisra aseeda.

I asked about some of the savoury dishes and discovered elmaraara made from sheep lungs, liver, and stomach with additional ingredients of peanut butter, onions, and salt. I have never been a lover of solid body organs, so it turned my stomach, especially as when I travel abroad for a long time, I profess to be a vegetarian, but despite that, I am happy to experience different cultures cooking traditions for research.

Next on the list of savoury foods was umfitit, and I wish that I hadn't asked about the recipe as it was sheep lungs, liver, and stomach with peanut butter and onions…the same ingredients as elmaraara but eaten raw. My stomach made another few acrobatic swings, and I didn't ask about any of the other savoury dishes.

Some of the other dishes that I dared ask about were moukhbaza, a dip made of bananas smothered with hot peppers, which, despite the odd combination for Western palates, was very nice, and kuindiong, a sweetened semolina welcome dish prepared by the Dinka people in Southern Sudan for guests. I was sure that it was a great treat, but since a similar dish had been served at my school for lunch, I had a loathing of the taste and texture, so it was obviously not my best day for a food tasting.

My plans for looking around the city suffered a big blow as the museums were shut on Monday. It is a major international conspiracy, as most museums around the world seem to shut on Monday. I had lunch in a hotel and afternoon tea in Gadhafi's Egg, a local nick name for the Corinthia Hotel, which is shaped like an egg and financed by Libya. I walked along the peninsular to stand on the bridge, overlooking the confluence of the White and Blue Niles. The waters are different colours, and the different coloured waters slowly mix as they travel downstream.

The Blue Nile had a lot more water in it than the White Nile after the recent heavy rains in Ethiopia. The force of the water in the Blue Nile had made the White Nile floods its banks. There was a lot of rubbish floating on the surface, and this had spread across the flood plain and would remain there until the Blue Nile water levels dissipated and allowed the weaker flow of the White Nile to resume and wash the rubbish away downstream.

I went back to the Corinthia Hotel for a cooked breakfast, as I felt like treating myself. After I had saved some cash by camping and slumming it, I often felt that I needed to splash out and enjoy some of life's comforts. Fried eggs and bread have never tasted so good, but there was no bacon or sausage. I got a taxi to the Ethnographic Museum for a quick visit, but I made sure that I was back at the Blue Nile Sailing Club to be on time for our planned 11am departure for the drive north.

After Khartoum goes north, the amount of rainfall decreases, and there is a vast expanse of desert. It is sandy and stony, with a few shrubs, but sometimes just sand as far as the eye can see. This was the fringe of the Sahara Desert, and it stretches for hundreds of kilometres northwards and thousands of kilometres westwards across the continent to the Atlantic.

That evening, we stopped at the Meroë pyramids. The city was the capital of the Kingdom of Kush for several centuries, from circa 800 BCE to 350 CE and whilst similar to the pyramids in Egypt, they have smaller bases and steeper sides so that they appear taller. All of these pyramids have lost their tops as an Italian 'archaeologist', but I prefer the term treasure hunter, who wanted to find treasure and rather than take the stones away one by one, he blew the tops off with explosives. This area was called Nubia by the Egyptians and was very rich in gold. It is possible that the Egyptian word for gold, nub, was the source of the name of Nubia.

Whilst we were looking at the pyramids, Gareth drove the truck around the outside of the site and parked behind a large dune for our bush camp. We had been told of the general direction that the truck would be, but it was a long walk, and the truck was not exactly where I thought it was, requiring a little further to walk in soft sand than I had expected. I felt some empathy for dozens of war films of people trekking through the desert, such as Tobruk! Or ice cold in Alex.

Once we had finally found the truck, our tents were quite spread out, as there weren't a lot of flat pitches in the dunes, and once you had found a pitch, you might still need to push some sand around to flatten it out a bit further to match the footprint of the tent.

We were up before dawn to walk back to the pyramids to see the sun rise and to see the pyramids in the early morning light. Unfortunately, the air wasn't clear, and rather than the sunlight creeping over the nearby hills and bathing the pyramids in bright sunlight, it just got lighter with no distinct light/dark line on the stonework as the sun rose. I had wanted to see the pyramid in darkness and, as the sun rose, to see the sunlight light up the tip and then work its way down the face of the pyramids as it rose higher into the sky.

We continued driving through the desert towards Wadi Halfa, but it will be several days as Sudan is a big country. After a long day of driving, Gareth drove off the road and almost immediately got stuck in some soft sand. We knew the drill, so we all got off, removed the sand mats, and wedged them under the wheels. Gareth gunned the engine, out of one soft patch straight into another. We picked up the sand mats and repositioned them.

The sand seemed hard, but it was only the top layer that was firm and supported a person's weight, not the truck. We would have to use the sand mats to get out in the morning, so rather than using the sand mats to get to our preferred location, we opted to camp here, but only after we had turned the truck around, so it was pointing in the right direction in the morning. The camp site wasn't ideal, but it would have to be done.

I used my pop-up tent for the first time in weeks. It is a small, lightweight tent that is basically a mosquito net, so it lets in a breeze, but there is no privacy. Its other advantage is that it is very easy to put up, and once out of its bag, it literally pops up by itself. The downside was that it had been stored for too long, and it had lost some of its spring. The fibre glass poles had a memory, and they didn't want to stay up. I thought that I had conquered its desire to refold itself, but in the middle of the night, it collapsed and gave me the fright of my life.

We were playing cards using the light from our head torches when our evening was disturbed by several camel spiders, large, fast-moving spiders, usually poisonous, but not all species are, but they are like mice to elephants. Zac finished the game standing on his chair to be sure he was out of their way.

In order to get back on the road, we had to use the sand mats that we wedged under the wheels. This time, once Gareth was moving, he used the momentum and drove all the way back to the road so that he didn't get stuck again. In the meantime, we picked up the sand mats and carried them back to the road before stowing them away and getting back on board.

The road follows the Nile, but where there is a large bend in the river, there is a short cut through the desert that saves some distance compared to following the river in a large arc. We stopped in Gondola, and there were several military fighter jets flying manoeuvres overhead. The only time we see military jets at home is at air shows, and we stand and wonder as they perform. In many other parts of the world, you cheer if you are a government supporter in a government-controlled area. Otherwise, you stare in dread and wonder if they are about to drop their bombs on you.

We stopped at the Temple of Mut and the Temple of Anut, and there were more pyramids, just like the ones we had seen in Meroë. We stretched our legs and went for a walk, but it was hot, and it was tiring walking in the sun on soft sand.

That afternoon, there was a dust storm off to one side of the road, and on the other side, some dark clouds were building, and the edges of the clouds were encroaching onto the road with a few raindrops falling. There were only a few drops, but it promised to get worse, so we hoped to outrun the storms.

We drove on and reached the Nile, a wide, muddy, but turbulent stretch of river in full spate after the rains in Ethiopia. The ground just here was rocky, and there was very little agriculture as it was too steep and rocky, just a thin ribbon of land near the river that had been cleared of stones and where water could be hand pumped up the bank and onto the fields.

We drove off the road into the hills and found a flat area to camp. We had outrun the rain clouds, but the sandstorm was still building on the horizon. The wind picked up and was blowing it towards us. I set up my tent at the bottom of a small wadi, hoping that the depression would shield it from at least some of the stronger gusts of wind. In a sandstorm, the dust gets everywhere, and there is no protection from getting a film of fine sand covering everything.

I had been in sandstorms before, and despite closing the doors and windows and lining all the edges of openings, with wet cloth, the fine sand still got into the room. You can taste the sand in the air. It gets up your nose and grates on the enamel of your teeth. Everything ends up with a fine layer of dust that takes several days to completely clear, as with every attempt to wipe it away, there is more dust thrown into the air to settle back again once you have swept, washed, and wiped every surface.

The downside of my decision to erect my tent at the bottom of the wadi was that there would be a reduced flow of air to keep me cooler, and I would have to move if it rained. But at least the tent pegs were easy to push into the sand.

As it was, the wind changed direction several times during the night and eventually changed direction completely and blew the sandstorm away from us, so we were spared. So, I have still not experienced camping in a sandstorm, but I was content to miss that experience. There were more camel spiders running through camp, and most of us ignored them except for Zac, who stayed on the truck out of harm's way.

Everyone was up early, despite breakfast not being until two hours after sunrise. So, we boiled water for drinks and took it easy, but we were still ready well before the allotted departure time. It was another long drive the day before we reached Wadi Halfa. It was a small town, and there was not much there. We searched for ice but couldn't find any. We tried several places, but they had sold out. I hailed a taxi to take me to the main ice plant. It was working, but it would not produce any ice for another half an hour. I was on ice duty with Noodles, so we had some freshly squeezed fruit juices whilst we waited for the ice to be ready.

Eventually the ice was ready, and I bought a large block and put it in the back of a tuk-tuk to get back to the truck. We cut it down to size to squeeze it into the coolers, but there wasn't much space for anything else.

Chapter 19
Cairo

I feel sorry for people who don't drink. When they wake up in the morning, that's the best they are going to feel all day.
Frank Sinatra

To get lost is to learn the way.
African proverb

Since Sudan is an alcohol-free country, another alcohol-related anecdote might be in order, and an alternative warning on bottles might read as: WARNING; The consumption of alcohol may create the illusion that you are tougher, smarter, faster, and better looking than most people.

Wadi Halfa is a border town, and we would be crossing the next day. The plan was to camp near the border so that we would be one of the first vehicles across in the morning and not get stuck in a long queue. We set off out of town and turned off the road into the desert. This would be a difficult crossing as they are very thorough and will really check the truck very closely and will scan all our luggage. Therefore, we had to empty our lockers and pack a day pack and a large bag as they expect travellers to travel with luggage, and it would be suspicious if we had none and left it in the lockers. They will also inspect all the lockers and pull everything out, so it is best for the lockers to be as empty as possible and neat and tidy to facilitate the process.

We arrived at 8.30am, but it was after 2pm before we were cleared, and the truck had been thoroughly checked, its papers checked, and it had gone through a giant scanner. It had also had its engine number checked against the carnet and recorded on their records for prosperity.

At last, we were through, and we drove down the road and to the ferry across Lake Nasser. This is the lake formed behind the Aswan High Dam. The Aswan

High Dam is an embankment dam built across the Nile in Aswan, between 1960 and 1970 in order to control flooding, provide increased water storage for irrigation, and generate hydroelectricity. It is 111 metres high, 3,830 metres long, and 980 metres thick at its base. The reservoir is 550 kilometres long, up to 35 kilometres wide, and 180 metres deep.

The ferry wasn't ready to go, so we splashed about at the water's edge and went for a swim. We didn't bother to get changed, we just dived in with our clothes on. It was hot, and we would dry in no time at all. Also, on the ferry were a bus, several cars, a cattle truck, and several goats with their feet tied and just left by themselves on the deck. It took nearly an hour to cross the lake before we docked at the town of Abu Simbel, famous for its temple of the same name. We drove off the ferry and into the town to find our hotel.

This was the first time we could buy beer, so we went straight to the bar. I had to swig out of the bottle and then go for a shower whilst there was still some hot water. There had been a lot of discussion after bush camping for several days in a dry country as to what would be first, a beer or a shower. Most people voted for a beer. It was never going to be a boozy night, as the beers were expensive.

We had a lovely hotel on the outskirts of the town. It was modern but designed to be a replica of the original local architecture, with domes, arches, stone floors, numerous courtyards, artefacts on the walls, cushions everywhere, and also air conditioning in the rooms and public areas. There was an option to visit Abu Simbel and see the light and sound show, but nobody was keen to go. However I have seen it, it is recommended, and you learn a lot about the temple for the hour that the show lasts.

Sometime before dawn, we drove to the temple and parked the truck in the empty car park. We were some of the very few tourists to actually stay in Abu Simbel. Most tourists stay elsewhere where there are better facilities and more things to do, and they are bussed in or arrive by plane for a day trip. The site opens at 5am so that you can watch the sunrise and light up the four 20-metre-high statues of King Ramesses II.

The twin temples were originally carved out of the mountainside in the 13th century BC, during the 19th dynasty reign of Pharaoh Ramesses II with construction of the temple complex starting in approximately 1264 BC and taking 20 years to complete. They serve as a lasting monument to the king and his queen, Nefertari, and commemorate his victory at the Battle of Kadesh. Their huge external rock relief figures have become iconic.

The complex was relocated in its entirety in 1968 under the supervision of a Polish archaeologist, Kazimierz Michałowski, on an artificial hill made from a domed structure, high above the projected water level of the Aswan High Dam reservoir. The relocation of the temples was necessary, or they would have been submerged during the creation of Lake Nasser and lost forever.

Work started in 1964 and took four years to complete. The entire site was carefully cut into large blocks up to 30 tons, dismantled, lifted, and reassembled in a new location 65 metres higher and 200 metres back from the river, in one of the greatest challenges of archaeological engineering in history. The recreation was so good that even if you know that it was cut into blocks, you cannot make out the cutting lines even up close. The complex was recreated on an artificial hill to give context to the giant figures. But on the tour behind the scenes, you enter the hill, and it is in fact a large hollow dome.

The sun rose, and people saw the first rays of the sun strike the giant statues. Not everyone wanted to go and visit the complex, so some had coffee in the café opposite the entrance, but soon everyone had seen as much as they wanted. We had a truck breakfast in the car park and then set off for Aswan.

The old road used to follow the Nile River in the valley, but since the creation of Lake Nasser, the new road takes a much more direct route across the desert from Abu Simbel, 290 kilometres, to Aswan. We reached some of the urban sprawl of the city a long time before the road dipped down towards the river and crossed a new bridge before turning to make its way into the city.

The must-do sights in Aswan are to marvel at the Aswan High Dam, the Temple of Philae, which, like Abu Simbel, was rescued from the rising flood waters of Lake Nasser, and the Unfinished Obelisk. That first evening in Aswan, I went with Noodles for a Nubian dinner at a private house in a Nubian village. We caught a river taxi from the stop on the river in front of the hotel, and it motored upriver past a couple of islands. It was functional but also interesting to see the city in the setting sun from the river.

We stopped on the far side and clambered out of the boat and up some steps to the village. There were an unbelievable number of shops and stalls in the market, but this is also a popular tourist attraction. We weaved our way through the crowds and then through some alleyways and found the right door. There were few windows overlooking the alleyways, but most of these houses are built around a courtyard, with the windows looking inwards, and no windows on the outside.

We were shown around the house, the various rooms, guest rooms, and communal rooms, all with tall barrel-vaulted ceilings, then the kitchen and bedrooms, and up two flights of stairs to the flat roof and a view across the roof tops and over the river to Aswan. It had simple furnishings and some prized family heirlooms, plus running water and electricity. Then it was time for the meal. It was prepared by the cousin of our local minder, Hajamona, consisting of potatoes in a piquant tomato-based sauce, a salad of tomatoes, onions, and cucumber, okra, rice, beans, and flat bread. It was simple but tasty and filling.

The next day, I walked around the city, taking in a few of the sights and trying to recognise some familiar places. The place has expanded since I was last here, and some of it I didn't recognise. However, I did find the public park that I had slept in a couple of decades ago, and it was just as I remembered. I also remember the open sand dunes on the far bank. There were some still around the edges, but there were many more buildings than before on the far side of the river.

The older buildings had an average height of about seven stories, but now there are ten and twelve new storey buildings. But there are still feluccas on the Nile, as I remembered, those distinct sail boats with triangular sails. Although I saw a few that were under sail, many now had motors and chugged up and down and danced with the small ferries crisscrossing the main river from side to side. I explored some of the older quarters near the river and ended the day by stopping for a meal at the upmarket Mövenpick resort on the far side of the river with views over the city from its restaurant on the twelfth floor.

We had booked a two-day felucca ride down the river. After breakfast, we packed our overnight bags to take with us and loaded our big bags onto the truck. There were two feluccas waiting for us at the pier opposite the hotel. Our first stop was just over the river on the other side, as the skipper needed to pick up some supplies and some extra ropes.

After that, it was time for a sail, and the two boats set off downstream. At the start of the first hour, there was a competitive rivalry as we egged our respective captains to go faster and overtake each other. But after a while, the wind died, the sails were furled, and we just drifted with the current.

It wasn't my idea for a couple of days of sailing, and I knew that there was a train option to get from Aswan to Luxor, and train travel has always interested me. Therefore, I planned to leave my companions 'sailing' which was more like just sitting in a boat whilst it drifted. We had moored near the bank for the evening meal, so I tested the depth of the water and waded to the bank, carrying my overnight bag above my head. I would drip dry as I walked back to central Aswan. We hadn't gone far, but it was a long way to walk, and no taxis or buses came past, so it took me a couple of hours to walk before I flagged down a taxi just outside the city limits.

I met Gareth for breakfast and accompanied him to the truck park. He had to get some papers stamped by the police, and I took the opportunity to drop off my sleeping bag and pick up my laptop. Then I bought a train ticket to Luxor and spent the day shopping and drinking coffee until the train was due to go at 15.00. I travelled first class for three hours for the cost of a sandwich back home.

It was not one of those spectacular railway journeys, but it was interesting to have experienced Egyptian Railways. The route followed the valley, and the scenery was rather unchanging, passing irrigated fields and date plantations. Often, it was fields on one side and desert on the other. The train was arriving late in Aswan and even later in Luxor but at least I had seen some more of the country from the comfort of a train.

I got off in Luxor and made my way to the hotel. I walked from the railway station through shopping streets and down to the river. I boarded a boat to cross the river. The ferry was old and crowded. It was slow. It was dirty. There were hawkers coming round trying to sell you things that you didn't want. Perhaps I was seen as rich, and they came over to banter with me and persuade me to buy whatever they had on offer, and some came back for a second or third try to sell me something. I just wanted to watch the banks as we motored across the river, but I was not going to be left alone, and I was continuously hassled by hawkers. It was the worst ferry crossing I have ever experienced.

I found my hotel, settled in, and waited for the rest of the group to arrive the next day. I was having lunch on the roof top terrace when I heard Nala turn the corner and park outside the hotel.

That afternoon, we had an orientation tour of the souk on the far side of the river. We needed a boat to cross, but there was a better option than the public ferry that I had taken the day before. There are plenty of boats moored at various piers that operate like taxis. They are frequent and cheap if there is a group of you and you have an idea of what the price should be.

The walk through the market wasn't as attractive as it could have been. There are a lot of traders, and they are more used to hassling tourists in several languages, so we were constantly being enticed by traders in a multitude of languages. I also had my foot trodden on by a donkey as it was whipped through the crowds by its owner, delivering goods to one of the stall holders, and it was painful.

I was kept busy exploring Luxor, where the top tourist sight is the Valley of Kings and Queens. Here are the remarkably well-preserved tombs of the ancient rulers and some very well-known names, such as Ramses II and Tutankhamun. The tombs have coloured paintings and hieroglyphics that still seem fresh even after 3,000 years. There are some artefacts to see, but most of them have been moved to the museum in Cairo.

After a long day of sightseeing, I got back to the hotel for a swim in the pool and to relax in the sun. But there was another day of sightseeing to follow. The Karnak and Luxor Temples were both within easy walking distance of the hotel and so iconic that all visitors had to make a visit. That evening, I went into town across the river with Sarah, Mat, Noodles, and Jacci to go to Kings Head, a traditional English pub with an English menu. It was just like a pub identical to any from the 1970s complete with atmosphere, as smoking indoors is still allowed in Egypt.

I was flying from Luxor to Hurghada, a coastal resort on the Red Sea, rather than go through more desert on the truck for two days. It was an early morning flight, and I was in the shower when there was some knocking on the door, probably waking everybody else up in the hotel. I wrapped a towel around my middle and answered the door to find the receptionist standing there to tell me that my taxi was here, half an hour early.

It was a long drive to the airport. We had to go up one side of the river, cross the river, and drive down the other side. Had I checked the maps and done a little research, it would have been cheaper and quicker to get a ferry across the river and then get a taxi to the airport. I was there for plenty of time, and there was little to do in a regional airport without many facilities.

I arrived at the airport in Hurghada on the Red Sea and caught a taxi to the hotel. This was just a small fishing village up until the 1980s when tourism took off. There are various water sports activities such as snorkelling, windsurfing, or scuba diving in the clear blue waters to see coral reefs and colourful fish. It is a major attraction for Russians, and they have a consulate here, and there are multiple signs in Russian.

I had a free day before the others arrived, so I booked up a windsurfing morning and a snorkelling afternoon. I was a scuba diver, and I would have liked to have gone diving. I was first introduced to diving in the Red Sea and was fascinated by the colours and shapes of the fish and the corals. It encouraged me to develop my skills, and I went on to go cave diving and explore shipwrecks. My major downside was that dive boats go out for the day to allow everyone to have a couple of dives, but I get bored, stuck on a boat for just two dives, and then have to wait to get back to shore. I had a great morning wind surfing, but the snorkelling in the afternoon was not that exciting and a long way from what I expected, but then I had been pampered with free food and drink on the boat.

I met the others in the group when they arrived later in the day. I was able to tell them about some of the better restaurants and places to avoid. I had some time with my fellow travellers, but I had already booked my flight to go to Cairo.

I flew into Cairo and took a taxi to my hotel. I went to search for a bar that was on the map but didn't exist on the ground despite walking around the block and the neighbouring streets…I had learnt that TIA and GPS pins on Google aren't so reliable in Africa.

I went to the Sheraton Hotel for an evening meal. The area also hosted the Russian Embassy, a heavily fortified police station, and the Kuwaiti, Saudi, and Libyan embassies, so security was tight, and it was probably the safest place in town despite being so near Tahrir Square, where there had been demonstrations during the Arab Spring. I crossed the square; it was just a big roundabout with a lot of history.

I tried an upmarket local wine made from the Bannati grapes, unique to the local Kouroum Vineyard located at El Gourna on the Red Sea. It was very pleasant and so much better than the Omar Khayyam and Obelisk wines that I had only been able to sample since arriving in Egypt. And the hotel had several other local wines that I was unable to savour as I had already bought the Kouroum wine.

And then it was a long walk back to my hotel and a chance to consider just how much I had spent. I could always console myself that it was expensive, but I was celebrating the end of my journey up the east coast of Africa. I had another week in Cairo to meet my fellow travellers and to visit the pyramids and the amazing Egyptian museum, but for me, this was the end of my journey from Cape Town to Cairo.

Other Books by the Same Author

The Klondikers

The Klondikers were the name given to the people who took part in the gold rush when they heard about the gold that was to be found around what was to become Dawson City. It was just sitting there, waiting to be picked up by anyone who could make the challenging journey to get there.

This is a recreation of the journey that one farmer from the wheat growing areas of the prairies around Calgary may have experienced to get to the gold.

It is the story of crossing the Rockies to the western seaboard, travelling up the coast, and making landfall. Then the intrepid potential gold panner had to cross the Rockies on foot, brave blizzards, and freezing cold.

When the weather and the ice had melted, he then had to paddle his way down 800 kilometres of river to the goldfields. Once he arrived, that was the least of his problems.

K2, The Savage Mountain

This is the story of travels in northern Pakistan using Gilgit as a centre. The journey heads westward to the fascinating Kalash Valleys and a surviving, unique culture struggling to live and maintain its identity in the harsh and rugged mountains bordering Afghanistan.

In the province of Baltistan and its capital, Karimabad, with its iconic forts of Baltit and Altit set high in the mountains, the route follows the infamous Karakoram Highway through the Karakoram Mountains that links the country to China via the Khunjerab Pass, the highest road border crossing in the world.

Looking eastwards, there is the Deosai plateau, which has an average elevation of 4,000 metres, and the disputed areas of Jammu and Kashmir. Finally, there is the ascent to base camp of K2, the world's second highest but most deadly mountain.

Overlanding the Silk Road

This is the long journey that follows the Silk Road overland between Europe and China. The journey starts in London with a dash across Europe. There is a pause in Istanbul to view its many treasures, and then the story winds through the history and countryside of Turkey. Then go over the border into Iran to experience its rich history and architecture.

There are bizarre experiences in the beautiful, modern, but empty city of Ashgabat, the capital of Turkmenistan. Just north of the city are the Dervasa Gas Craters, located in the middle of the desert, with their secret spectacular display best seen at night.

A trip to the disappearing Aral Sea is followed by an immense amount of empire building, architecture, and history across a land fought over by Alexander the Great, Tamarind, and Genghis Khan, to name just a few of the conquerors who have roamed across this landscape.

There is an enchanting wander through the mountains of Kyrgyzstan. This country of beautiful mountains and lakes is known as Asia's little Switzerland.

The scene slowly changes as the Muslim influence gives way to Han Chinese dominance, the Great Wall of China, and the end of the Silk Road at the ancient capital of Xian and its famous terracotta army.

Yellow School Bus

This is a trip from Anchorage in Alaska to Panama City in an iconic yellow school bus. There is a wild frontier landscape in Alaska, a glimpse of the Klondikers story of panning for gold in the Yukon, and always with the potential danger from bears, moose, and elk.

Travelling through the United States roughly following the Pan American Highway, there are stops at some of the most famous national parks, such as Yellowstone and the Grand Canyon, to name just two of many. There are side trips to Antelope Island and Salt Lake City and a stop off in Las Vegas for the glitz.

A nostalgic ride down Highway 66 relives some of the past, and there is a visit to the meteorite crater outside Flagstaff. Over the border into Mexico, there is some relaxation on the beach and a taste of tequila.

The journey twists through Aztec and Mayan culture, over crocodile infested rivers, and an oasis of English culture in Belize in an otherwise Latin American environment. There is relaxation on Caribbean islands, hunting for sloths, tasting the high life in spas, and some romance as the journey weaves its way through the mountains, history, and wildlife of Central America.

Crossing Russia on the Trans-Siberian

Russia is a vast country that covers more than a third of Europe and stretches for nearly nine thousand kilometres across northern Asia. The journey takes the reader on a tour through Russian culture, history, and geography, starting in the Imperial City of St Petersburg with its spectacular palaces and museums.

A voyage by ship leaves St Petersburg to follow rivers and canals, crossing several lakes through the northern pine forests past wooden cathedrals and monasteries, to join the Volga to reach Moscow. The Kremlin and Red Square are plus many other sights, including one of the largest and ugliest sculptures in the world.

Moscow is one of the longest railway journeys in the world on the Trans-Siberian railway, passing through birch forests, over grassy steppes, and through the Ural Mountains.

There are stops enroute at Yekaterinburg, where the Imperial family were murdered by the Bolsheviks, horse riding in the Altai Mountains to reach Mount Belukha, Siberia's highest mountain, and at Irkutsk, near Lake Baikal with its unique biodiversity and the world's largest volume of fresh water, before finally reaching Vladivostok in Russia's far east port and its Pacific.

Across the Caspian

This is a tale through the Caucasus, from Europe's lowest point on the shores of the Caspian Sea to its highest point on the summit of Mount Elbrus. The route follows a strand of the Silk Road from Ashgabat, the capital of Turkmenistan, through the desert to reach a ferry across the Caspian to Baku.

From there, the journey winds through some of the history of the Caucasus, with its ancient kingdoms and the landscape of Azerbaijan, and across the border into Georgia. This country is famous for its distinctive and good quality wines, plus a large number of churches and monasteries, an enclave of Christianity surrounded by populations that are predominantly Muslim.

Mount Elbrus is in Russia to the north, but the border was shut so it meant a diversion through Cappadocia in Turkey before approaching Mount Elbrus from the Russian side of the border for the attempt on the summit, which at an elevation of 5,862m is Europe's highest mountain.

Condors over Chile

The condor is associated with the Andes, and this story recalls travelling down the length of the Andes and the search to see condors. From the far north of the continent on the arid Guajira Peninsular, the route passes through hotspots such as Medellin and Bogota and a climb up Mount Puracé, an active volcano.

There is a break in Quito to stand on the equator. It is a fascinating visit to the Galapagos and a voyage through the islands that make up the archipelago. There is a huge array of wildlife that is not afraid of humans, so you can get really close to its tortoises and its other unique wildlife.

Then there is the experience of seeing some of Peru's ancient civilisations and the country of origin of more than 3,500 varieties of potato before continuing down the Andes to the windswept wastelands of Patagonia to Ushuaia at the end of the world in the search for the condor.

Gold, Ivory and Slaves

Travelling down the west coast of Africa, there is a lot of history and how wealth was made for merchants out of the misery of Africans captured and shipped across the Atlantic to be sold into slavery. The triangular trade involved shipping European manufactured goods to Africa to buy slaves to ship to the Americas and then trading them for tobacco, sugar, and rum to sell in Europe.

Many of the countries didn't exist as states and were known by the products they produced, such as the Pepper Coast, Ivory Coast, Gold Coast, and the most emotional name, the Slave Coast.

Slavery was eventually banned after more than 12 million Africans were sold into slavery. But then came the Scramble for Africa, when European powers sought to grab as much African land as they could before one of their rivals got there first. It wasn't slavery, but it was economic exploitation, sometimes of the worst type, and arbitrary borders decided by Europeans in Europe without regard to local realities. And then there was independence, and the people were exploited by their own leaders. Is it any better today?

Carnival

Starting at the southern tip of the continent in Ushuaia, the adventure goes through the windswept plains of Patagonia and past settlements whose immigrants from Wales brought their language and customs with them. The Patagonian plains give way to the Pampas before reaching the major urban centre of Buenos Aires for some culture and relaxation.

The journey of 1,200 kilometres northwards reaches the magnificent, thundering Iguazú Falls on the border of Argentina and Brazil and then crosses into the jungles of Brazil. There is a lot to explore in the Pantanal area of wetlands to see piranhas and capybaras before heading to Rio de Janeiro for the extravaganza and colour of the carnival, the biggest party on earth, and everyone is invited. But Brazil is a big country, and there is a lot more to see and explore before reaching the Caribbean coast of South America.

Reflections on El Camino

El Camino is the pilgrim's route across northern Spain to reach the cathedral in Santiago de Compostela, which was built on the site where St James' body was buried after he was martyred in Jerusalem in 44 AD. His remains lay unmarked and unknown for eight centuries until a miraculous light led a shepherd to discover the bones in a cave.

A cathedral was built over the spot where the bones were found, and it became the destination to reach for pilgrims in the mediaeval era. But the route to Santiago de Compostela was fraught with danger for those pilgrims, with notoriously bad weather in the Pyrenees, warring kingdoms in the north, civil war, and the ever-present danger of invasion from the Muslim Moors who controlled the southern half of the Iberian Peninsula.

This is a long-distance walk through the countryside, culture, and history of the area from St Jean Pied de Port on the French side of the Pyrenees to Santiago de Compostela and onwards to the Atlantic coast of Spain to finally Finisterre at the end of the world for the known Roman Empire after a walk of 900 kilometres. But what is the route like today for the modern pilgrim?

A Message from the Author

Whether you have enjoyed the book immensely or found it a useful aid to insomnia, please provide me with a little help and feedback. Amazon Books algorithms work to advertise books that they think would be of interest to other readers based on their search criteria. But they only work well if they have sufficient data, which means at least fifty reviews on the Amazon Books website.

Therefore, in order to help a struggling author, may I ask you to write a review of this book on Amazon Books? It can be of any length, but I am not looking for a five-hundred-word review, just rate it honestly as you think fit and write what you felt about the book. You can use your own name or remain anonymous by using a pseudonym. Thanking you in anticipation, Norman Handy.

Back Cover Story

Starting out in Cape Town, South Africa, there is plenty to see as the journey heads north. The scenery changes from green fields and vineyards, such as Stellenbosch, to the deserts and giant sand dunes of Namibia. The desert changes to savannah only further north. There are numerous safaris to see wild animals in their natural habitat, including hippopotamus, the most dangerous animal on the continent, and cheetahs.

There are close encounters with elephants in the Okavango and views of thousands of zebras before crossing the border in Zimbabwe. There are the magnificent Victoria Falls and a railway journey across the Zimbabwe countryside to Bulawayo, with its great industrial centre and railway heritage.

On safari through the Serengeti and the Ngorongoro Crater, visitors have the opportunity to see all of the Big Five game animals, the five most dangerous animals to hunt on foot. There are the Spice Islands, the Bwindi Impenetrable National Park, where there is an opportunity to walk with gorillas, and plenty more countries and experiences to enjoy, and this was still only halfway up the continent to Cairo.